Sowing the First Harvest

National Reconstruction in Guinea-Bissau

by Ole Gjerstad and Chantal Sarra[illegible]

Sowing the First Harvest

National Reconstruction in Guinea-Bissau

Published and Printed by

LSM Information Center
P.O. Box 2077
Oakland,CA 94604 USA

first printing - 1978

ISBN 0-919914-29-2
printed in USA

Table of Contents

Preface

This collection of articles and interviews is one product of our three-month visit to Guinea-Bissau in early 1975, at the invitation of the *Partido Africano da Independencia da Guine e Cabo Verde* (PAIGC) and the country's Ministry of Information and Tourism. We wish to thank our comrades in both the Party and the Government for their friendly advice and cooperation, and hope that this small book will be a first contribution to having made their efforts worthwhile.

Some of the chapters have previously appeared in the Tanzania *Daily News*, *LSM News*, and other periodicals. The final compilation and editing, as well as the production of the book, has been done through the collective efforts of the staff at the LSM Information Center. Together we dedicate this book to all those men and women who, throughout Guinea-Bissau, continue their lives of hard work, sacrifice and political struggle to expand the revolutionary experience of humankind.

O.G.
C.S.

Introduction

For a long time Guinea-Bissau was a place we knew only through intermediaries. In the years since Liberation Support Movement (LSM) started to work in solidarity with the national liberation movement, the PAIGC, we had translated and published much of the movement's own materials; we had read practically every book and article on the subject, seen several films, talked to PAIGC militants abroad and led discussions and workshops on the topic of the struggle. So we felt we had a good idea of what would confront us when, in early 1975, we arrived in Bissau for a three-month visit at the invitation of the new PAIGC Government. Still, we kept cautioning ourselves; it seemed easy enough back there in California or Quebec, New York or Minnesota when with just conviction we defended the armed struggle and described life in the liberated areas as if we had grown up there. Reality had to be different - harsh and complex; no rose garden, no tea party.

As with so many young political activists in Canada and the United States, our involvement with anti-imperialist work goes back to the late 1960's. The surge of guerrilla campaigns and revolutionary people's wars in Africa, Asia and Latin America fired the imaginations of the alienated youth of the imperialist countries and produced the idols of countless study groups and college essays: Che, Cabral, Ho... A new dimension entered our lives and we looked to far-away places for guidance and inspiration in dealing with contradictions and social problems we didn't quite understand. Romanticism? Escapism? No doubt, there were elements of both, and in any case, for most it proved to be little more than another fad, a way to enrich one's life before the more prosaic concerns of degrees, jobs, and monthly payments imposed themselves with full force.

It was during this period that the 'forgotten wars' in Portugal's African colonies gained wide-spread attention among progressives in the Western world. By the time the anti-war movement and the torrent of political activity that came with it reached its crest, PAIGC controlled nearly half of Guinea-Bissau. The colonial forces were isolated in the towns and scattered pockets of the territory while reports told of a new society with strong socialist elements taking shape in the liberated regions. At about the same time, the speeches and articles of Amilcar Cabral, the PAIGC Secretary General, were published abroad and quickly established this African patriot not only as the forceful leader of a small and struggling people, but as a brilliant revolutionary theoretician whose message reverberated far beyond the borders of his colonized homeland. For Cabral and his Party comrades, as for many of us abroad, the liberation of Guine was but a part of a world-wide struggle against capitalist oppression and exploitation; their victory would take us all a step further on the road to a world where the welfare of the masses, not power and profits, is the motive force of human creative activity.

This vision became the *raison d'etre* for many of us, in LSM and in other groups, who worked to raise political and material support for African liberation movements. The revolution in 'Portuguese' Guine no longer belonged to the Guineans alone; it had become part of a more universal human experience. It built on the already accumulated lessons of earlier liberation wars and revolutions and pushed the frontiers still further back. It gradually became clear to us that revolutionary nationalism in the so-called Third World would come to deal severe economic blows to international capitalism and also be a source of rising political consciousness among the peoples of our own countries. Struggles like that of the Guinea-Bissau people would help undercut the material privilege of the imperialist countries and rip the veil off the more innocuous welfare state-type exploitation. They would at once expose imperialist plunder as a major basis for Western 'affluence' and serve as a source of inspiration for those here at home who felt that 'there is nothing we can do' in the face of the almighty establishment. It would give a wider perspective to all those caught in the labyrinth of never-ending local and community issues. In this way revolutionary solidarity work plays an important part in laying the basis - both objectively and subjectively - for stronger revolutionary movements within the capitalist metropoles themselves. By contributing to the efforts of liberation movements like the PAIGC, by practicing proletarian internationalism, we effectively work toward our own liberation.

The conviction that our aims were the same helped make up for the remoteness of the African peasants and guerrillas who were facing conditions so vastly different from our own. Though European presence in Guine goes back five hundred years, it was only at the end of the 19th century that Portuguese colonialism moved to effectively control the small and swampy territory which the 1884-85 Berlin Conference had left for it to exploit. But Portugal, itself a semi-feudal and economically subservient country, did not have the conquering capacity of its colonial colleagues and as late as the 1930's, tribal resistance wars were still fought in several regions.

Throughout the colonial era, the economic basis of Portugal's presence in Guine remained narrow. Unlike the larger Portuguese colonies to the south, Angola and Mozambique, the West African climate and topography made White settlement a difficult enterprise and hundreds of administrators, traders and would-be settlers succumbed to fever and other tropical diseases on expeditions to the hinterland Heavy taxation, forced labor on government projects and forced cultivation and exchange of rice, peanuts and other cash crops became the means by which the Guine peasants were made to repay colonialism for its 'civilizing' mission.

No settlers, only a few plantations and less than a million subsistence-farming peasants to suck dry; with such a limited source of profits the Portuguese did only what was strictly necessary to maintain their crude form of exploitation. Bissau remained a small trading port, few roads were constructed and no industry was built whatsoever. Social services such as education and medical care were nonexistent for all but the two or three thousand government servants and merchants who lived off the extraction of wealth from the African people. Even Catholic missions were largely kept out of the territory until the final period of colonial rule.

This process did not facilitate much integration of Guine's population into the ways of the colonizers. The majority of the country's inhabitants are of animist, chiefless ethnic groups, like the Balanta and Manjaco, for whom colonial penetration resulted in nothing but impoverishment and brutal oppression. Their huts, animals, children and even spiritual ceremonies were taxed; their crops 'bought' for a nominal price and their labor power expropriated arbitrarily by the European overlords. About one-third of the population belong to Islamized groups, like the Fula and Mandinga, which pushed into the territory from the North and East about one hundred years ago. Their chiefs and religious hierarchy at times collaborated with the Portuguese in suppressing the rest of the people, a relationship that for some continued into the recent liberation struggle. A small group of mulattos from the Cape Verde Islands, also occupied by the Portuguese, inhabit the towns as traders or civil servants.

While Britain and France effectively turned large parts of Africa into appendages of their industralized economies and raised groups of Black caretakers in their own image before reluctantly accepting African independence, Portugal's own backwardness prevented her from 'modernizing' colonial exploitation in this way. A few monopolistic trading companies grew fat on Guine's wealth, yet were incapable of advancing beyond their outdated mercantile capitalist stage. The colonial fascist state, too, built on an alliance of landowners, merchants, bankers and the Catholic church, remained locked into its archaic doctrines. As new flags were hoisted in African capitals and most of Western Europe donned the garb of social-democracy, the Portuguese ruling classes resorted to increasingly oppressive measures in their fight against the advance of history. In the metropole, the anti-fascist opposition was outlawed, jailed or driven into exile. In the colonies, the nationalist aspirations of the people were considered as treason and dealt with accordingly, forcing the few politically conscious African intellectuals to abandon petitions and other peaceful protests for clandestine and more militant forms of resistance. 1956 saw the formation of PAIGC and the Popular Movement for the Liberation of Angola (MPLA), while in Mozambique several exile groups joined in the Mozambique Liberation Front (FRELIMO) six years later. Their combined activities brought escalating colonialist repression, causing temporary setbacks but long-term political gains for the movements, a dialectic that was to lead to the outbreak of protracted people's wars.

In Guine the real turning point came in 1959 when fifty striking dockworkers were massacred by the police at Bissau's Pidjiguiti pier. From this event Amilcar Cabral and his comrades concluded that urban protest of this kind would remain isolated and ineffective; that only by force and with the participation of the masses of the people would Portuguese colonialism be brought to an end. While Cabral himself set about the task of politically training small groups of PAIGC cadres in the shelter of the neighboring Republic of Guinea, others left for the countryside, secretly travelling from village to village, persuading the peasants that the time to throw off the colonial yoke was rapidly approaching and that they, the villagers themselves, were the ones to do the job.

The years of preparation gave PAIGC the strength to launch the armed struggle on 1 January 1963. Within six months the Portuguese were expelled from large regions of the country and already in 1964 the liberation movement held its first Congress inside the country. There they resolved to begin building a new society in the liberated regions while they were fighting the Portuguese forces. Military struggle was seen only as the highest expression of political work. Mobilizing the population, engaging them in the administration of the liberated parts of the country, developing self-sufficiency and providing for basic social needs became the essence of the liberation struggle. The establishment of bush schools and clinics, rudimentary 'people's stores' and even democratic village tribunals to replace the colonial 'law for the indigenous' enabled the masses of the Guinea-Bissau people to see beyond the immediate hardships and sacrifices of the war and gradually define for themselves why they were fighting and what kind of independence they wanted. Their military victory was only a question of time. 'We have already won the war,' Cabral said after the 1964 Congress.

The last-ditch efforts of the Portuguese could only postpone the inevitable. The regime's legal measures of colonial 'autonomy' were a farce and their sudden concern for the social welfare of the Africans remained irrelevant to the vast majority. Their cowardly assassination of Cabral in 1973 resulted in the increased determination on the part of his comrades who shortly thereafter went on to proclaim the free Republic of Guinea-Bissau from the liberated heart of the country. Finally, on 25 April 1974, under the combined pressure of the three liberation wars, the Lisbon regime collapsed and a new era opened in the history of both the Portuguese and the colonized African peoples.

Our stay in Guinea-Bissau, from March-June 1975, took place at a time when the PAIGC Government was still in the early stages of reorganizing the life of the nation. Less than six months had expired since the departure of the colonial troops and administrators. Left behind was a chaotic bureaucracy, an economy in ruins and a bewildered urban population who in large part had been living off the colonial war machine. To us outsiders, the problems seemed at first overwhelming. The hard-working Party cadres were less intimidated, though nobody tried to hide the difficulties in setting the new nation on its track. Undeveloped, ravaged by war, but with the majority of the population mobilized behind the revolutionary movement, what options are open to a new country in this situation? This was the obvious question as we moved around the territory on our mission of collecting life histories of peasants, townspeople and guerrillas who had in one way or another participated in the liberation struggle.*

The articles and interviews on the following pages are intended to convey the framework in which that question is presently being answered through the day-to-day work of the masses of the Guinea-Bissau people. We have not been able to present a full picture of their efforts, and important areas of work, like health care, have been left undocumented. Yet we hope that our central conclusion will be conveyed: In their task of building a new society, now as during the liberation war, PAIGC and the people of Guinea-Bissau continue to advance our common horizon in the struggle for a world without exploitation. Our duty, within the imperialist countries, remains to contribute where we can, assimilate the lessons and utilize these on our own front of struggle.

---

* A volume of these stories will be published by LSM Press in the coming year.

Aspects of a Difficult Transition

Suddenly emerging from colonial underdevelopment and the destruction of a long and bitter war, the people of Guinea-Bissau face many difficulties in consolidating their independence. But despite the desperate shortage of cadres, the ruined economy, and the sharp city-countryside contradictions, the contours of a new kind of people's democracy are already visible.

It is the middle of the dry season but still hot and sticky. The tin-roofed terminal building feels like a Turkish bath and by the time we have been cleared through customs, all our energy seems to have drained through our soaking wet shirts and underwear. The luggage is positively leaden. To our relief we find a jeep waiting. The aging vehicle and driver both bear signs of long years of service under the Portuguese, though a fresh coat of yellow paint and a new set of khakis indicate that each has somehow made a fresh start.

The open ride soothes the body and clears the brain. On one side of the road the tall, dry grass periodically gives way to fields and small clusters of huts. Scattered palm trees turn into forest a few hundred yards off. The soil is dusty and dark red as are the walls of the mud huts. It is still early in the day and many people seem to be heading for town. Across the road, grim barbed wire strung on eight-foot high concrete poles seals off the sprawling camps which up to six months ago housed part of the 35,000 colonial troops sent here to hold PAIGC at bay. Now most of the area is abandoned, with various pieces of dilapidated equipment strewn about in open spaces. Only as we approach the town do we see guards posted and signs of activity in the long rows of white-washed barracks. At a road-block we stop for a brief exchange in melodious Creole* between our driver

---

* The commonly used hybrid of Portuguese and local African languages.

and the youth on duty. From the shade of a canopy, four or five FARP* militants follow us with their eyes as we move off in a protesting second gear; non-Portuguese Whites are not a frequent sight yet, even here in the capital.

The Legacy of the Past

We are not sure what to expect in Bissau, the colonial stronghold in this overwhelmingly rural country. It was here, among the wage workers and those whom Amilcar Cabral later identified as 'the revolutionary petty bourgeoisie' that PAIGC recruited many of its key cadres - like Nino, Chico Mendes and Osvaldo Vieira - in the early years. Pidjiguiti and subsequent waves of arrests made clandestine work extremely dangerous, but after initial setbacks the trickle of militants leaving the city provided the liberation movement with some of its key cadres.

As the armed struggle progressed, conditions in Bissau became increasingly difficult. Masses of refugees swarmed into the city to escape the acts of war that destroyed their villages, herds and crops. But escape to what? With its population swelling from about 25,000 in 1961 to perhaps three times that number during the course of the war, the capital had little to offer but a life of misery and destitution in its crowded *bairros*, the African quarters built in distinct separation from the Portuguese part of town. Housing and food grew scarce while corruption flourished correspondingly. The price of meat went up tenfold over a period of five years and traditional staples such as rice and corn periodically disappeared completely from the shelves as larger and larger areas of the food-producing regions fell under the liberation movement's control. Portuguese troops filled the streets and bars while violent crime, theft, prostitution, alcoholism and drug abuse transformed the once calm trading port and its inhabitants.

Despite the great problems, the Party continued clandestine work in Bissau throughout the war. On the one hand, its militants faced brutal repression: time after time, often using infiltrators, the PIDE ** would get on the trail of PAIGC cadres as they were spreading propaganda and mobilizing people for the struggle. Hundreds met imprisonment, torture and death at the hands of the colonial regime. The other aspect of the regime's 'carrot and stick' tactics included psychological warfare to turn Bissau's inhabitants against the liberation movement. Endless radio propaganda, political rallies with

---

* The People's Revolutionary Armed Forces, PAIGC's army.
** International Police for the Defense of the State; the fascist Portuguese secret police.

mandatory attendance, the creation of war-related jobs and Spinola's promises of 'a better Guine' had their effect. Most steadily employed Africans depended directly on the Portuguese for their living: 2,000 worked in the shipyard alone and thousands more for the army. Yet, from the crowded *bairros* any Portuguese could pick up an African servant for ten dollars a month.

The question of jobs was in fact an important one since without proof of 'valid' employment Black men were conscripted into the colonial army. Volunteers were indeed very few until General Spinola, colonial Governor from 1968-1972, started to grant rank and higher pay to certain specially trained Guinean troops in an effort to 'Africanize' the war. He conceived this plan to serve two functions: first, to split the African population and, second, to relieve some of the pressure on his own demoralized troops in the field. Toward the end of the war this corps of about 600 *comandos africanos* was usually to be found in the front line during major battles, suffering and dying in the swamps at the hands of their fellow Africans - only to delay the inevitable.

Spinola's 'better Guine' scheme also included plans to upgrade the standards of the already privileged group of urban Africans, mainly government functionaries and those employed in the service sector. In lieu of a true national bourgeoisie, the General perceived the need to create a cushion of assimilados* to stand between the colonizer and the masses of the colonized - a tiny elite to somehow cover up the cruder aspects of exploitation but completely serve the old master. Salaries were increased, the civil service inflated and educational opportunities improved, if not on a grand scale, then at least in clear contrast to the past practices of Portuguese 'ultra-colonialism.' This new petty bourgeoisie, in true style, rapidly adopted the habits and values of the colonizers, moved into the 'civilized' part of town, substituted Scotch and martinis for *kana*** and palm wine and took in every third-rate western or karate show in Bissau's only movie theater. 'Cabral can promise anything - only Spinola can provide it' was the regime's motto.

How deep did this process go? Sensing our expectations, our host, Manuel Santos (Manecas), veteran guerrilla commander and now also the country's Minister of Information, takes care to brief us on conditions in the city. In his early thirties, tall and broad shouldered and wearing jeans and a checkered sport shirt, he completely defies our image of a Cabinet Minister. His office is new, but simple; only a humming air-conditioner reveals the status of its occupant.

In a brief vacuum between the withdrawal of the Portuguese

---

* Africans who qualified as 'civilized' by colonial standards.
** A potent sugar cane liqueur.

forces and the full arrival of the PAIGC, Manecas explains, a wave of violent crime and theft left Bissau almost a replica of the Wild West towns people know from the movies. Now, six months later, the worst has been brought under control. Immediate measures include an all-out campaign against drug abuse, through both educational programs and the introduction of stiff sentences. In fact, a law to apply capital punishment to pushers is being prepared. Many of the prostitutes, brought across from the Cape Verde Islands, have disappeared with the troops, and local 'business' seems to have all but dried up. Theft has been countered by a combination of legal and political measures, which include interviewing convicted thieves, under full name and address, on the weekly 'Wake Up!' radio program. The shame and embarrassment to the culprits and their relatives has helped cut the rate of theft by two-thirds. Right now the Government is busy preparing action against black marketing and speculation particularly in foods and foreign exchange. Colonialism and war has so distorted the economy of this potentially rich agricultural country that in Bissau, many essential foods are still imported and retailed at prices only the wealthy can afford.

It is a sobering picture Manecas paints. He is encouraged, however, by the results of the Party's work so far. Thus armed, we are better able to appreciate, over the next few weeks, the many contradictions facing the city and its inhabitants at this stage of the reconstruction process. Yet, at times we cannot avoid being taken aback - sometimes amused, sometimes perplexed or even demoralized. Western 'bourgeios' values seem well entrenched. There are super-flare bellbottoms, platform shoes, Jimi Hendrix t-shirts. Along the wide *Avenida Amilcar Cabral*, stretching from the former gubernatorial palace and down to the Pidjiguiti pier, teenagers lounge with soft drinks, beer and whiskey in the sidewalk cafes. The lousy movies draw huge crowds, much larger than some of the political rallies we attend. The colonial heritage is still present in full force.

Non-Portuguese foreigners are few and highly conspicuous. Cuban and Eastern European diplomatic staff and technicians are in the majority. The handful of Western 'experts' can be found at the Pidjiguiti Hotel, formerly a hostel for high-ranking military personnel, while they wait for apartments or assignments somewhere in the countryside. The Swedes dominate, but there are also a couple of British and American UN officials. Those with experience from the fun life of the international expert circuit appear genuinely disappointed. 'In this place,' sighs an overpaid economist recently arrived from Rio, 'you either work your ass off or get out.' Which is maybe not such a bad idea after all.

Many of the Portuguese merchants seem to have stayed. So far they have suffered little from the new regime but have still taken care to transfer as much of their wealth abroad as possible. The final transfer of power last September was preceded by a virtual hemorrhage of money and valuables destined for the coffers of Portugal and Switzerland. Who knows what the future will bring? In the meantime, they are unwilling to abandon what has sometimes taken them decades to build up and, besides, their troubled motherland is hardly the place to go if worried about socialism and class struggle. In any case, they are cagey toward strangers and stick mainly to their own in the lower part of town, cramped between the walls of the old fort and the palm-lined waterfront, where their houses, shops on the ground floor and apartments above, are separated by narrow cobbled streets. Tanned, furrowed faces, eyes frequently bloodshot from large amounts of sunlight and alcohol, they have enjoyed opportunities unequalled in the metropole. How, they wonder, will the new Government go about settling accounts? In the evenings, they enjoy a game of cards and a drink outside, or at most a stroll under the deep green mango trees up toward the hospital and Grand Hotel where other Portuguese, mainly teachers or remaining civil servants, congregate on the cool porch. Nostalgia is thick in the air as they eat their dessert banana with knife and fork and reminisce about what used to be. Liveried barboys stand by, ready to move at the slightest sign - eight hours a day, six days a week, forty dollars a month.

Still, even in this environment which on the surface appears hermetically sealed off from the struggles of the *bairros* and the countryside, signs of the new times are obvious enough. Old street names, those of famous Portuguese explorers, generals and missionaries have been painted over and replaced with the names of fallen liberation fighters and African patriots like Mondlane and Nkrumah. Colonial monuments have been knocked down leaving only cement foundations and twisted iron bars. In the two or three small bookstores, among the color magazines and James Bond in translation, we spot a few slim Marx-Engels selections, books on Cuba and China, Mario Soares' autobiography and stacks of *Afrique-Asie* magazine.

But most of all we notice the FARP militants. With their AK-47s ready, friendly but alert, they guard all public buildings and strategically important spots. Their uniforms still represent a varied selection of Portuguese left-overs and donations from friendly countries, but with their vigilant posture, their modern and well-kept weapons, there can be little question as to their effectiveness. The vast majority are peasants and strangers to city life; many have spent years in the bush and first set sight on the capital six months ago when they arrived to take over from the Portuguese. A strange experience, perhaps; the street lighting and tarmac roads contrast sharply with the traditional *tabanca* village and the people's mentality is vastly different. But while in the past the urban population would have been inclined to show contempt for such provincials, their attitude is now one of uncertainty - half withdrawal, half deference. FARP's presence is a reminder that the revolution has reached even these inner quarters of the old system and that real changes are on the horizon.

'To Live Better and in Peace'

'Always keep in mind that people are not fighting for ideas, for the things in anyone's head. They are fighting to win material benefits, to live better and in peace, to see their lives go forward, to guarantee the future of their children.' Amilcar Cabral's message conveys the essence of Guinea-Bissau's revolution as we experience it over the next two months in the interior of the country. The contrast with the city is striking. At the center of it all are the people, human beings whose main concern is their food, houses, families - their daily lives, here as in any other part of the world. Ninety per cent of Guinea-Bissau's population are peasants and, by our standards, their needs seem modest: to get enough food and decent shelter, to see the fruits of their hard work and to bring up their children in peace and the traditions of their ancestors. But under Portuguese colonialism even this was impossible and it is here in the villages that the crude and super-exploitive nature of this system fully came into its own. Merchants bought the peasants' rice, peanuts and palm oil and paid as they saw fit; the Portuguese administrators and their African *cipaios** enforced the terms of trade, collected the dozen different taxes and rounded up 'free' native labor when needed. Later, the army arrived to help out. 'Development' was confined to what was strictly necessary in order to carry out these operations, with schools, clinics and even missionary work being kept to a minimum.

Such life circumstances made revolt a reasonable option for the Guinean peasants. Their forefathers had fought the Portuguese and memories of pre-colonial times and resistance were kept alive. But the spark had to come from without. Illiterate, parochial and firmly anchored in centuries-old traditions, they were by themselves unable to challenge 20th century colonialism. It was for the PAIGC to unshackle their potential. 'We were so tired,' the men and women tell us again and again. 'We worked hard but the *tugas*** took all we had and treated us worse than animals. When the Party asked us to fight, we looked back and found we had nothing to lose.' The initial fear and skepticism of many gave way once the first guerrillas had proved that they were in fact capable of defeating the enemy, thus exploding the myth about the invincibility of the Whites and giving the population a sense of confidence and dignity which colonial rule had done so much to suppress.

This was the beginning of a new era in the people's history. With clinics and schools in the liberated areas the narrow horizon of tribal existence began to expand. Along with growing contact and interaction across ethnic lines, a new awareness of other nations, countries,

---

* Administrative police, usually Africans.

** African word for Portuguese soldiers.

continents emerged. In order to sustain the protracted struggle the peasants had to break the fetters of backwardness, gain knowledge of the contemporary world and reorganize village life in line with the new demands. The exigencies of armed struggle turned the revolt into revolution. Life in the liberated areas was by no means easy as Portuguese forays and bombing raids destroyed houses, crops and livestock and forced people into the bush on constant alert. But it brought a vision of what life in a free Guinea-Bissau could be like; a vision that little by little became part of reality as PAIGC's zones expanded and the quality of life there improved. The movement's capacity to act on Cabral's words ensured the popular character of the struggle and gave it a significance that would not evaporate with the final departure of the colonial forces. Today, with the Portuguese gone, the peasants' main concern is still to improve their daily lives - rebuild their villages, plant new crops, restock their depleted herds. From experience they know that success will depend on their own hard work and that today's efforts will go toward a better tomorrow. The peasants remain both the force and the aim of the revolution.

We have arrived in the south-western region of Tombali, the largest of the country's eight administrative regions. With us is Fernando, our interpreter who is also responsible for facilitating our work. Fernando was born in Bissau but brought in Dakar, Senegal, where he acquired his impeccable French, a high school certificate and a great love for rock music and lazy days on the beach. Following the example of his older relatives, he joined the Party in 1973 and worked at its Boke supply base in the neighboring Republic of Guinea. He has little more experience in village living than we do and to the Tombali peasants he must appear almost as strange, hidden under dark glasses and a giant, sweet-smelling Afro.

The scars of war are everywhere. PAIGC effectively controlled most of this region since 1964, but Portuguese troops held on to a number of posts from which they guided the bombers to their targets and periodically launched raids to terrorize the population. Heaps of bricks and burned logs in old village sites bear witness to their accomplishment. On the edge of the forest, the undergrowth is only now recuperating, embracing with fresh green tendrils the charred trunks where one year ago Fiat jets dropped their loads of American and Canadian-made napalm. Empty ammunition cases, rather than rocks or sand bags, are used to protect against rainy season floods. Guiledje, Guadamael, Bedanda - the battles fought here - will no doubt get their space in the country's future history books.

The Tombali State Committee, the leading political-administrative body of the region, has picked Tchugue village to be our base. We arrive with an entourage of two political commissars and two FARP militants one scorching noon, all covered in dust after an hour's bumpy jeep ride from the administrative center of Catio. The air shimmers over the open fields, stretching for miles on both sides of the muddy Balana River which corkscrews its way from near the eastern border to the Atlantic, slicing the region in two. Groves of mangos and the occasional palm tree rise from the ocean of dry grass. From the distant forest, columns of thick smoke rise vertically before dispersing to a greyish, motionless haze. All over, fields are being burned in preparation for the planting season. Women with baskets of rice on their heads and children struggling under heavy bundles of firewood step aside and wave as our driver carefully maneuvers the Russian-made jeep along the deep tracks, now dry and hard but almost impassable once the rains start. Half way across the open stretch we are greeted by a barbed wire fence with a battered sign: *Zona minada!* (mine zone) painted in red on a skull-and-crossbones background. A quarter of a mile further on, on a slight ridge, we pass a derelict observation post and two abandoned artillery positions before reaching the first huts. Yapping dogs chase the car with small boys close behind, almost lost in a cloud of red dust. We pick up quite a tail and by the time we come to halt by a row of tin-roofed huts, a group of villagers are already waiting.

Tchugue's five hundred inhabitants are of the Balanta ethnic group, the largest in Guinea-Bissau. Originally settled in the north-central Nhacra district, the Balantas started migrating about a hundred years ago, particularly toward the South and along the large rivers where they could grow their rice the way their ancestors had done for generations. As they moved, they took the names of their old *tabancas* with them - those from Tchugue in the North built a Tchugue in the South. The chiefless Balantas came to know the Portuguese through colonial trade, taxation and forced labor. They resented their masters, but felt powerless in the face of the colonial machinery. As a people they never accepted their subjugation but knew from experience how the Portuguese reacted to manifest opposition.

The early PAIGC organizers found a ready audience in some of the highly respected Tchugue *homen grandes* (elders) and through them reached the rest of the population. Yet mobilization was no less dangerous here than in the city; once the Portuguese got wind of what was going on they responded in predictable fashion and in Tchugue alone fifteen villagers were killed on suspicion of working for the Party. By that time, however, the armed struggle was already starting and in late 1963, the merchants and colonial troops were driven from Tchugue with heavy losses, though not before they had destroyed much of the *tabanca*. What they left undone, the bombers later finished. Life in liberated Tchugue was by no means easy but, used to great heardships and encouraged by PAIGC's advance, the people did what the situation demanded. Only a few fled to neighboring Guinea or sought the relative calm of the Portuguese-held towns. The vast majority stayed in the PAIGC areas where, after all, they could grow enough rice to feed themselves. With the *tugas* and all their taxes gone, there was even a small surplus to be exchanged for cloth, soap or other essentials at the People's Store which was established in the nearby forest only a year after the Portuguese left. Embryonic medical care was provided by the local FARP units or at the Guerra Mendes bush hospital some four miles away. And through its elected *tabanca* committee the Tchugue people, for the first time in decades, came to play a decisive role in shaping their own destiny.

While on the strategic defensive, the colonial troops used terrorist tactics against the liberated areas. Tchugue received more than its share of NATO bombs and napalm and in 1968 the Portuguese flew in commandos by helicopter to again destroy the *tabanca*. The population managed to escape, but by the time the troops retreated, five freedom fighters lay dead and many huts were in ashes. This attack was led by Fuab na Digna, the colonialist-appointed 'chief' who before the war ruled Tchugue like a conquering warlord, exploiting people's labor and confiscating their crops at will. When the Party first attacked, he fled with the Portuguese and went on to become an officer of the notorious *comandos africanos*. Never did we encounter such hatred and bitterness among the people as when the subject of Fuab, the 'exploiter,' 'traitor,' and 'murderer' came up. He is now in Catio jail, waiting to be brought to trial before one of the newly-created People's Tribunals.

Still the Portuguese were not through. In early 1972, in a last desperate move to stem the tide of liberation they reoccupied a number of Tombali villages, including Tchugue. First came the paratroopers, then the helicopters and river craft. They dug trenches and underground shelters and lined the *tabanca* with mines, barbed wire and machine gun nests. They set up long-range artillery and mortars in order to control the surrounding area. In the fresh cement of the bunkers they carved their names: Miguel Figureido, Joao da Costa, Paulo Lopes. . . . Many were to leave only in coffins as patrols were wiped out in the bush and hardly a week passed without a PAIGC attack. Open craters and collapsed shelters testify to the intensity of the war here.

For most of the demoralized *tugas* life in a place like this was pure hell, and so they welcomed the Lisbon coup no less than did the Africans. 'Jose' Kassem, the Lebanese-born merchant and supporter of the Party, remembers 25 April very well: 'When I heard of the coup on the BBC news, I grabbed a bottle of brandy and went to see the Portuguese captain. We poured two solid ones and I raised my glass: 'To your early return to Portugal.' He looked at me. 'Watch your mouth.' When I told him the news, he wouldn't believe me - it wasn't until the next newscast that he could hear for himself. The whole camp was jubilant. From that moment on the troops hardly did anything but sit around and drink beer. Our militants could walk openly right into the *tabanca.'*

We climb out of the jeep to curious stares; visitors are rare, let alone a group like ours. The two commissars are shaking hands all around. Kau Sanbu, lean and strong, his dark eyes always alight in the shade of a wide-brimmed Cuban bush hat, was a sidewalk tailor in Bissau when he joined the Party in 1957. He worked underground here in the South for three years before the war and knows the countryside like the palm of his hand. Despite his position - he works at the PAIGC Secretariat in Bissau - he remains at heart a villager. Apart from a brief mission to Conakry, he has never been out of the country. His colleague, Sana Tchuda is in his mid-twenties. He was recruited when PAIGC units first arrived in his village and, still an adolescent, sent to bush school. After five years of schooling, and between his assignments as teacher and political worker, he spent a year in the USSR for 'general political instruction' and, recently, three months in Eastern Germany for a course in public administration. Sana is now the political *responsavel* for Catio district. A man of few words, there is an aura of calm and great patience about him which makes us feel at ease and well looked after. Sana in turn introduces us to a husky, middle-aged man in khaki suit and brown *cofio* cap. He is Sambis na Iuk, chairman of the village committee. Together we walk across the blazing hot open space, past the row of bombed-out colonialist shops, to 'Jose' Kassem's house where Fernando and the two of us are to be lodged.

Life at Tchugue Village

Over the next few weeks, at the tape recorder taking life histories, over cups of *kana* or by glowing fires in the clear nights, we get a glimpse of what the liberation struggle has meant to the people of Tchugue. On the day after our arrival Sambis calls a meeting of villagers and there, amidst screaming babies and the general disorder of foraging pigs, chickens, goats, and fighting dogs, we are established as 'comrades from America, friends of the Party,' who 'want to tell the people in their country about the Guinean revolution.' Striving for simplicity, we try to explain LSM and the specific purpose of our mission, but are far from sure how to transmit North American reality to this colorful assembly in the shade of a giant mango tree. The real burden is with Sana who provides the Balanta version. He talks for at least twice as long as we did while we watch with anxiety the expression on people's faces. It is hard for us to read their reaction, but Sana must have been convincing; as soon as he is done, one of the *homen grandes* limps into the semi-circle, greets us and starts in a squeaky voice, waving his hands toward the crowd on whose behalf he is speaking. 'We are glad and honored that you have come such a long way to work with the people of our *tabanca,* you who are friends of our Party and our people. Unity and friendship between your people and ours is important and we will therefore do all we can to cooperate in your work. Thank you.' The meeting ends with applause and a salvo of viva's for the Guinea-Bissau revolution and international solidarity. That evening we are presented with a pig and two chickens as a reinforcement of the old man's words.

In Tchugue, as in the other villages we are to visit later, daily life centers around reconstruction. Behind the structure that used to be the Portuguese army workshop a small group of men are making bricks. The pit from which they take the solid clay is by now a good six feet deep and the stuff is handed up in buckets, mixed with water and shaped by hand before being left to bake in the sun. Rows and rows of bricks which are good for a hundred years if kept from getting wet; something which is nearly impossible, when the flood gates of heaven open wide in July and August. This brick-making crew would normally produce enough for the entire village, but this year demand is too heavy; every *moranca** is adding at least one structure and some are being rebuilt from scratch. Yellow straw, neatly cut and bundled, stands ready to make the roofs. A new and bigger People's Store is going up by collective efforts to replace the present one which is temporarily located in an old Portuguese army hut. The cadres in charge arrived immediately after the Portuguese pull-out last September, together with a teacher and a medic. The Portuguese clinic was taken over as it was and a school was installed in what used to serve as the troops' dining shack.

From dawn to dusk we see men and young boys carting logs and bricks along the village trails. Huts are materializing at a forced pace; in about six weeks the rains will be here and all efforts will then have to be turned to the rice fields which almost encircle the village. The women are presently bringing in the remainder of last years' crop. Most of Guinea-Bissau's rice is produced in the paddies of the southern and western regions where the many rivers and annual floods ensure a good yield, given the primitive method of cultivation. A short-handled hoe is the universal implement, whether for rice or the smaller plots of peanuts, corn, and manioc set on higher ground often within the village itself. Even last year the Tchugue fields yielded a surplus of about one hundred tons, most of which is still in the overflowing granaries waiting to be shipped to hungry Bissau. The more they can produce this year, the less the country will have to import, and with a great lack of food in certain areas, every ton counts.

With overgrown fields to be cleared and thousands of refugees yet to be resettled, President Luis Cabral has declared it the country's aim to regain the pre-war level of food production within three years. Even if difficult to achieve, the President's appeal has struck a positive

---

* Group of huts belonging to each extended family.

note in the countryside. Whatever else may be lacking, we find no shortage of determination. Even in our initial naivete we had somehow expected to find a certain resignation in the war-torn areas - after all, some of these people are rebuilding their homes for the third time in a decade. And there must have been times in the past when it seemed that the destruction would never end. Still, confidence, not resignation, is now the prevailing mood. Independence means continued hard work, long hours of toil in the fields and *morancas*, much like in the past. But the difference is in the incentive. 'From now on, we ourselves will reap the fruits of our work.' Families who fled their villages during the war have started to return and the Government is inundated with requests for seeds and tools for all those who are starting anew.

The immediate challenge is to achieve self-sufficiency in foods as rapidly as possible. In the longer run, increasing agricultural production implies changing to more productive methods of cultivation and introducing new equipment and fertilizer to improve present yields. This, of course, is as much a political as a technical question since the very structure of village life is derived from the techniques people use to eke out a subsistence from the waters, fields and forests around them. In the northern and eastern regions, for instance, most staples are still grown by 'slash and burn' cultivation. Here a conversion to new ways has become a necessity, not only due to low and unreliable yields, but also because increasing population pressure may soon lead to a shortage of land with the past practice. Starting next year, the Government will restrict the amount of forest that can be burned for cultivation.

But permanent fields and new kinds of crops, with the introduction of fertilizer and irrigation may demand a new approach altogether. How will the land be redivided? What will be the new division of labor? How will the needed equipment be acquired and who will run the processing plants the Government wants to set up soon? Will we see an updated system of individually worked plots or will the emphasis be on collective efforts? And if the latter, how will production be organized and how will the surplus be used? The answers to these and similar questions will be of great consequence to the future of Guinea-Bissau, to what kind of social system, what brand of socialism, the liberation struggle will have given rise to.

The war has uprooted much of the old ways and given PAIGC a tremendous prestige among the rural population, opening the way for more far-reaching changes than have been tried in most other African countries. On the other hand, enough of the past remains to make it evident that, without the famous spark from without, the peasants will resurrect old customs and practices as much as possible. A coherent agricultural policy - as part of a larger development plan - will therefore be essential if the tremendous surge of the revolution is to be carried on and deepened.

That cooperation will form a prominent element of the new regime's approach seems clear enough; the key task is to find those forms which will provide the best transition from the old ways. Certain kinds of collective work exist in the traditions of the various ethnic groups, but all of them, including the Balanta with their extensive use of communal labor, also have well developed notions of private property and individual wealth which cannot simply be ignored. Yet, to leave such notions unchallenged as the peasantry becomes increasingly integrated into the new national economy, will almost certainly mean a backsliding away from the socialist objectives of the PAIGC. A path must be found which, within a framework of preserving the gains of the liberation struggle and consolidating the people's power, can meet the primary economic demands of the new nation. But the enormity of this challenge does not really sink in until later when, back in the capital, we are able to discuss some of the questions involved with Party cadres.

For many Americans and Canadians, collectivization and socialism conjures up visions of forced migration, prison camps or worse. The process we witness in Guinea-Bissau has taken a different course. Considering, on one hand, the central role of the peasantry in the liberation struggle and, on the other, the 'mental decolonization' still to be done in the towns, the countryside will no doubt remain both the base and leading sector of the revolution for the foreseeable future. This demands that the close interaction between the masses and the leadership can be carried on and that the tendencies toward bureaucratic commandism and technocracy, which will inevitably make themselves felt as the new state apparatus finds its *modus operandi,* can be checked. The struggle for a revolutionary state will require mass participation no less than did the people's war, and for this reason the organs of people's power - the village committees, tribunals, local militia - retain their function: to explain and help implement Government policy at the local level and, inversely, articulate the views of the village population to the administrative cadres in the offices of Bissau. Perhaps the present role of these can best be compared to that of a filter: the initiative is with the leadership, but by the time an idea or a proposal has been properly discussed at the local level, it may have been substantially modified or even rejected. In this way the masses are brought into the decision-making process. If the present trend continues, they will more and more come to assert their strength, first on the issues directly concerning their daily lives, later on a wider range of issues as well.

Thus, the question of formulating agricultural policy, for instance, is not left to agronomists and functionaries far away in the capital, but is discussed at length, again and again, in *tabanca* meetings across the country. At the meetings we attended, the peasants express their views with a directness and divergence of opinion that completely defies the 'awkward class' image imposed on them by Western anthropology texts. We find the same spirit at the annual Popular National Assembly (ANP) session in Bissau where one hundred twenty deputies gather to establish the overall political framework for the country's progress over the next year. What we had initially suspected might be just a rubber stamp affair turns into heated debate and the session finally takes up eight full days instead of the planned four.

Determination to move ahead, the tremendous will to learn, confidence in the future ..., at first we feel overwhelmed by the force of this process that seems to permeate every fiber of the society around us. Pieces of our vocabulary - 'revolution,' 'masses,' 'people's power,' - terms so easily used by every self-respecting *politico* in our part of the world - are given substance and pulled down from the realm of abstraction. We want to store up on inspiration and pass it on to friends and comrades back home. Are we ever going to see something similar among our own people? What lessons can we learn from the people of Tchugue and their compatriots? What seems to us so infinitely complex is to them quite simple: 'We were so tired. . . . Now we ourselves will reap the fruits of our work.'

Such are our thoughts as we say goodbye to Sambis, Jose and other friends in Tchugue and climb into the slender *pirogue* (dugout) which, submerged to within a few inches of its edge, takes the lot of us across the unruly Balana River. A last salute to the tiny receding figures on the far bank and we are off to a place, across the rice fields and through the forest, where a truck is waiting to take us to our next destination. Fernando, on hopeless platform shoes, makes up the rear, lugging his guitar case while at the same time trying to keep his Afro from collapsing with sweat and the ungentle touch of thorns along the narrow trails. Kau hums a traditional tune and the FARP comrades reminisce about their encounters with Portuguese troops in the surrounding bush as we make our way toward the rapidly setting sun.

To Mobilize the Masses

The small lantern casts a dim yellow glow which barely reaches the corners of the room. A rack on the wall holds a few tin plates, mugs and a canteen, and in an open closet opposite hang two sets of well-worn camouflage fatigues. By the door, next to the jar for drinking water, hangs the omnipresent AK with four spare clips in a belt slung over the barrel. We are seated on the single bed with 'P.A.I.G.C., AMOR, A.S.' in elaborate red, blue and green embroidery on the spread. Across the table Silva is putting our skimpy Creole to a test. He speaks slowly, using facial expressions and imaginary designs on the wax cloth to make his points. When the subject is combat or vigilance, he slaps the revolver on his hip for emphasis. Apparently we are the first foreigners to visit the tiny Porto Gol garrison since PAIGC's arrival and Silva, who is the local political commissar, badly wants to talk, to find out about the world yonder. We, too, have many questions, but with no interpreter within reach we are confined to the very elementary. Long periods of silence follow each attempt at discussion while Silva shakes his head in sad resignation.

We are here by sheer accident. On our way back to Bissau from three weeks in the northern regions, we made a detour to drop off a comrade who has a week's leave to help his family move their belongings from a bush shelter back to the *moranca* they left eleven years ago when the war came to their village. The 'road' has in fact been closed since then and years of floods did not leave us much. Open mine craters made the journey no easier. You'd want to curse those who built the road so badly in the first place until you remember that every single rock, every ounce of coarse gravel was carried from afar by the men and women from the villages along the route, Cubadjall, Malafu, Enxale, sweating for no pay under the *cipaio's* whip. The driver, eager to reach the main road before dark, had the rest of us hanging on to the seats, the canopy, anything, just to stay inside the jeep. Finally, the driveshaft broke a couple of hours' walk from Porto Gol.

From the yard the wide Geba estuary looks like black velvet below us in the moonless night. What used to be the Portuguese *chefe do posto's* office is in the middle, shelf after shelf packed with old volumes of *Boletim Cultural da Guine Portuguesa* and dusty legal documents. A pile of cardboard boxes contain tax registers from decades back, all in laborious longhand listing name, size of household, how much paid and how much owed. There always seemed to be something owed. The buildings have bullet marks, some going back to 1963 when a PAIGC unit under the late commander Caetano Semedo drove out the Portuguese. The *chefe* just fled in his boat, leaving behind his African wife and their children. The merchant Rendeiro, on the other hand, a skilled hunter, put up a fight before being captured with his arsenal which provided Caetano's group with its first machine gun. The liberation movement, however, did not yet have the capacity to control the region and so, here too, the *tugas* returned in force and dug in. Everything is here as they left it - the perimeter of barbed wire, trenches and machine gun nests. The *chefe's* house is connected to an underground shelter. From the huge piles of rusty cans we gather that the troops never ventured far to dump their garbage.

The legacy of Portuguese occupation has given Silva and his four FARP militants enough to do. One of the soldiers, N'Famara Dabo, who was brought up in Gambia and speaks a little English. explains that they are still struggling against the effects of colonialist psychological warfare. The Party will need both time and patience to gain

aleones! Abaixo ao opportunistas burgueses!' 'Down with the chameleons and bourgeois opportunists!' Under these slogans the Party is venturing to expose those who go through a change of face merely to retain their privileges and dodge the genuine change of mentality which the transition to a socialist society demands. Merchants, professionals, office workers, teachers - many among them were deeply involved with the old regime and will change only as far and as fast as they are forced to. Often in positions of influence, they will represent a danger to the continued revolution unless their true stand is brought into the open.

The Need for Cadres

The administrative experience of the PAIGC leadership stems mainly from the war and their work in the liberated areas. The huge workload they now confront is made even heavier by the novelty of the peasant situation; the liberated countryside in conditions of war is a far cry from today's independent State with its intricate machinery. Few important issues can now be dealt with on the spot as was com mon during the armed struggle. Complex coordination, budgeting and long-range planning are required and there are areas of work with which few militants are familiar, such as tourism, diplomatic services and industrial development. The near complete lack of data in all sectors has made it difficult for the Government to bring itself up to date with the current state of affairs and work out a comprehensive development plan. In the meantime, refugees keep returning, epidemics periodically threaten an already precarious, though improving, health situation and food shortages must be alleviated. While, during the war, all support took the form of donations and Party militants received only food and uniforms, today the Government must find cash and credit to pay its thousands of employees at home. Contradictions arise where the immediacy of such issues imposes itself on the already beleaguered administration. Instant solutions are demanded, emergency measures applied and resources, already designated for other use, reallocated to plug the holes. Cadres whose main task should be to chart long-range development programs, are at times left scurrying from one emergency to another.

Perhaps it could be no different at this stage, less than one year after the final take-over. Where present programs are direct follow-ups on efforts from the armed struggle - for example the educational system or the People's Stores - results are impressive. In other areas, like the resettlement of refugees and the expansion of public health services, concrete plans exist and are being implemented. As for the country's overall economic development, only the vague contours are visible so far. Agriculture will remain the basic sector for the forseeable future with related light industries like food processing, tanning and forestry to be established in step with increasing production. Assistance from abroad is at this time centered on the mapping of natural resources by teams of agronomists, foresters, geologists and fishery experts roaming the territory. A prerequisite to any substantial industrial development is the improvement of communications, primarily the construction of more and better roads and bridges. No private enterprise is involved; all cooperation is with governments or international agencies such as the UN specialized sub-organs.

Here, again, efforts from the time of the liberation struggle have given the new regime a head start. With a wide basis of international support, it is in a far better position to diversify its external links - and thus consolidate its independence - than were most other African countries at liberation or, for instance, Cuba fifteen years ago. Close links have been retained with Portugal under the MFA and the Lisbon Government provides teachers, medical personnel, scholarships and credits to cover urgent imports. Similar agreements have been signed with the German Democratic Republic, Sweden, Cuba and the Soviet Union, and during the time of our stay, North Korean, Algerian and Egyptian delegations arrived for the purpose of working out assistance programs. An agreement was signed with China for an interest-free loan to be used, with the assistance of Chinese agronomists, for the further development of rice cultivation along the Geba River.

That these countries, which all supported the PAIGC during the armed struggle, should become Guinea-Bissau's first international partners is no surprise, even if, in line with its firm policy of non-alignment, the Government announced its openness toward relations with any country on the basis of mutual respect for national sovereignty. Apparently, the only offer to have been turned down so far was a rather vague promise of financial help from the US Agency for International Development. No investment code has yet been elaborated, though it would be safe to predict that the new rationale will be fundamentally different from the colonial one which left a brewery, built for the sake of perspiring and demoralized Portuguese troops, the country's only industry worth mention.

Among the many tasks which today face the PAIGC Government, two are of particular importance. First, since foreign personnel will no doubt play a major role in national reconstruction for years to come, a coherent and clearly defined framework for their participation must be established. The building of a socialist society will require both comprehensive planning and active intervention by the State, the lessons from other African countries show what disastrous effects foreign participation, not only by private corporations, can have if not integrated into an overall development plan. The experiences of countries such as Cuba and North Korea, whose situations are similar to that of Guinea-Bissau, should be of help in the elaboration of such a plan.

Second, new cadres must be trained. The presence of expatriate workers, even if qualified and friendly to the regime, does not reduce the importance of training more Guineans. In the initial six months after the Portuguese departure, the new regime faced a critical shortage of humanpower. Unlike Mozambique, Guinea-Bissau had no period of transitional government to prepare the final take-over and the colonial bureaucracy actually continued to function until broken up and reorganized after PAIGC's arrival in Bissau. The Party's experience with the skeletal state apparatus in the liberated areas since the proclamation of the Republic one year earlier, enabled it to fill most top posts from within its own ranks and the paramount considerations in forming the new Government were clearly political. Thus all the members of the State Council (the Cabinet) are also on PAIGC's leading bodies and a few have also retained their positions on the FARP General Staff. Of the four members on the top PAIGC Permanent Secretariat, only the Secretary General, Aristides Pereira, is not a member of the State Council.*

In practice, therefore, the Government is an arm of the Party with a few dozen leaders holding prominent positions in both. This concentration, explains Julio de Carvalho, (better known as Julinho) FARP Political Commissar and a veteran Party leader, has been forced upon them by the contradictions of this period. 'On the one hand we have the comrades whom we trust completely, but who do not yet have much experience. On the other, are the functionaries who served in the colonial administration. They have plenty of administrative experience, but can we trust them?'

There is no instant solution to this contradiction: to train cadres takes time. It will be years before the new educational system will produce a full crop and even the 600 youth who are abroad for training will not be ready for some time yet. Most Party militants with secondary education or higher have been set to work in the various Government departments, both to learn the job and to act as political catalysts to the Portuguese-trained staff who will now have to be re-educated. It will be for the new mass organization, particularly the UNTG, to establish new attitudes toward work: a spirit of collectivity and a sense of responsibility toward the masses and one's fellow workers. In some departments, regular work place discussions with criticism and self-criticism are now engaging the employees in this difficult business of transformation, bringing the deeper meaning of the revolution home to many who, left to themselves, would have preferred to bury their heads in the sand and continue in the old

* Aristides Pereira has since been elected President of the Cape Verde State Council. The other three Permanent Secretariat members are Luis Cabral, Francisco Mendes (Chico Te), Prime Minister, and Joao Vieira (Nino), Minister of Defense.

groove.

While this process grinds on, a massive load of responsibilities rests with the small group of leading cadres. Administrative duties which under normal circumstances should have been delegated, are now frequently left with the leaders themselves. Time that might have been spent in supervising the work of others and tracing the lines of the country's future, is often occupied with day-to-day work details. 'We work night and day just to keep things going, ' says Julinho. 'I myself have so much to do that I seldom get time to sit back and really think about it all.'

While the pressure of work is not likely to subside as time goes by, the PAIGC leaders seem determined that they will find more opportunity to devote themselves to their political duties as the reorganization of the state apparatus makes progress and the administrative bottleneck is forced open. The regional State Committees do most of the local work and serve to link the leaders with the grassroots but this is only a partial substitute for the direct interaction which was so crucial in giving the liberation struggle its revolutionary momentum. During the war, in the bush and the sheltered forest villages, the peoples daily concerns were part of the leaders' lives as well. The better such a relationship can be maintained, the greater are the chances for the Guinea-Bissau revolution to retain its popular character.

Much hinges on the Party cadres and the impact the liberation struggle has had on them personally. For those of *assimilado* background - and in the top echelons there are many - this is perhaps a particularly critical moment. 'The most important struggle right now is with ourselves. Now we'll see who went through a *real* transformation in the course of the war, and who simply managed to stay afloat with no basic change in their values.' The comrade who is speaking has himself been facing serious contradictions since he returned to the capital last September. To carry on the struggle in the bush he had to suppress many of the needs and values acquired in the staid family home in downtown Bissau. The war taught him to sleep without shelter, to go days on end in the same wet uniform, to suffer hunger when there was no food. For the first time he learned to know the peasants of his own country; he shared their rice and millet, he picked up enough of the vernacular to learn something about their customs and traditions. The kind of people who had been servants back home became his comrades in the struggle. By living and fighting with them, his old class values were slowly giving way to new ties of common interest and identity.

Today a Government post has taken the place of the army and an air-conditioned office block has replaced the bush and makeshift shelters. Due to the nature of our comrade's work, a car and a pleasant house - both taken over from the colonial administration - have been put at his disposal. Since the Government also needs the services of his well-educated wife, housework and child care are left to a woman servant. His new work load is heavy and entails frequent trips abroad and so he has hardly been able to visit the countryside to witness the progress of reconstruction. It disturbs him to find how easily he has readjusted to this kind of life and how far removed the bush and the villagers all of a sudden have become. But for the memories of the past, they now enter into this work mainly as figures to be compiled in so many files and ledgers.

It is only logical that PAIGC, like most comtemporary national liberation movements, was started by a group of urban and relatively well-educated *assimilados*: only such people had the opportunity to catch the currents of anti-colonial thought which swept Africa after World War II and link this up with their own direct experiences. But for this group of 'revolutionary petty bourgeoisie' to effectively lead a mass movement in a rural country like 'Portuguese' Guine, they had to transcend their past. The struggle required that they objectively and subjectively align themselves with masses of people from backgrounds very different from their own. They had to, in Cabral's words, 'commit suicide as a class.' The demands of the armed struggle forced this process on many of the militants, like our comrade above.

Just as the war was only a first step, the fight against old class values must continue. It is a lifetime task. Those who fought in the bush will have to carry on, often in the face of a resurrection of their past life style. Those who do not have this basis, whether they were students abroad or joined the movement after 25 April, confront an even more difficult task. In their situation we often recognize the paradoxes and contradictions which would-be revolutionaries like ourselves face in our day-to-day lives and work within the capitalist metropoles. Like them, conditioned by a system we want to eliminate, we constantly feel the pressure of 'the enemy within': the pull of material rewards, the need for immediate gratification in the work, the tendency to promote oneself at the expense of the collective or to pursue individual interests rather than what truly serves the cause of the struggle. Like us, these cadres can only succeed by engaging in a constant struggle with themselves and their comrades, by adopting a vigilant posture toward their own weaknesses and always remaining open to criticism by others. In the struggle to create a new man, they must be the first to discharge some of their ballast. Only then can they, little by little, really implement the PAIGC cadre's watchword: 'Serve the People.'

The pressures of the current period demand near Herculean efforts on the part of all Party workers. In many ways, this is a critical time since the early steps in the reconstruction process cannot easily be reversed. The shortage of qualified cadres, the need for an immediate increase in food production, the necessity for agricultural reform -

what is the correct approach to these problems? One set of solutions could reinforce the powerful trend toward a bureaucratic and technocratic socialism; another could promote the struggle for a continued mass-based revolution with 'politics in command.' As PAIGC knows, a reliance on temporary and piecemeal measures, pragmatic and expedient in the face of great needs, would almost certainly lead to the former path. The latter and perhaps more difficult option will demand a comprehensive approach by which material advances go hand-in-hand with ideological struggle, by which the creation of a 'new life' is also the creation of a 'new human being.'

Is this possible? Considering the tremendous practical problems, is it not a luxury to talk about ideological struggle? How can we even talk about socialism in view of the ponderous tribal traditions and 'backwardness' that dominates large parts of the Guinea-Bissau population? Before independence, the PAIGC would avoid the labels 'Marxist' and 'socialist' in describing the way they went about liberating and rebuilding their country, yet the content of their actions was clear enough. This content has retained its essence; theirs is a socialism shaped by the needs of liberation and embodied in the structures set up to carry out the continuing struggle. But just as the revolutionary process is now entering new and unknown ground, so is the mold of the nation's future still in its fluid state. There are many lessons to be learned from the construction of socialism in other 'Third World' countries as well as from the painful experiences of independent Africa. But, in many ways, together with FRELIMO in Mozambique and MPLA in Angola, PAIGC is breaking new ground. Amilcar Cabral, in his theoretical works as in his leadership of the liberation struggle, did more than anyone else to chart the early stages of this long process. For his comrades-in-arms to carry on, they will need every bit of creative energy that his leadership and their common experiences have left them.

Wherever we visit, in the *morancas* under reconstruction or in the reorganized Government departments, we are greeted by the same message: 'We haven't had much time yet. . . . Give us a chance, come back in a few years.' We find problems, sure, but also confidence and determination. Building on the results and experiences of the armed struggle, the people of Guinea-Bissau are now working to advance the revolution still further. In their efforts they will draw lessons of value far beyond the frontiers of the country itself. Near the end of our three months, when we wonder aloud how best to convey what we have seen and learned, Kau gives us his parting advice: 'We have little need for praise. Only critical observation and discussion can help us over the hurdles that block the path of our progress. If we indeed are comrades in a common struggle, then this should be your contribution.'

His words linger in our minds as the Bissalanca runway disappears behind us. The rivers are swollen with the early rains and the late afternoon sun makes the water in the furrows of the long paddyfields shine like strands of silver thread. With their backs bent, smaller and smaller as the ancient Air Senegal Dakota hesitantly rises toward the clouds, the peasants below are just starting to plant the first crop of rice in fully liberated Guinea-Bissau.

'Since Pidjiguiti We Never Looked Back'

Joao Emilio Costa now works for the Bissau Port Administration. In 1959 he was part of the Bissau dockworkers' strike that ended in a bloody massacre at the small Pidjiguiti pier where 50 workers were killed and over a hundred wounded.

When I started working at the docks in 1949, conditions in Guine were difficult. Many people were without work and food was always short. Our wages were almost nothing and the work hard, but we were glad not to be starving and accepted it, more or less.

This began to change after several years. More and more Africans became aware of what colonialism was doing to our country and tried to improve the situation. At the dock we formed a club to collect money and send youngsters to study in Portugal. But the Portuguese didn't like it and one administrator, Augusto Lima, tried to stop our activities. There was also an African worker by the name of Joao Vaz who always spoke against what we were doing. Some people in the club weren't dockers; Rafael Barbosa, for instance, was a construction worker and Jose Francisco, a sugar cane worker. They were both active in the Party and so were Caesare Fernandes, Jose de Pina and Paulo Fernandes who worked with me. But this was something very few people knew at the time.

Most of us worked for the big Casa Gouvea company,* either on the dock or on boats taking goods to and from company shops all over the country. But with our low wages, life was becoming more and more difficult. The basic wage was only 10 escudos (approximately 40 cents) a day. In 1959, after much discussion in the club and at

---

* Part of the giant Compania Uniao Fabril's empire.

work, we finally decided to ask for higher wages.

The manager was Antonio Carreia who had just left his post as colonial administrator to work with Gouvea. Well, he refused even to listen. Of course this was the first time in Guine's history that workers united to confront their bosses. So, Barbosa and Augusto Laserde said that we had to go on strike and show them we were serious.

On 3 August we all gathered at Pidjiguiti, about 500 men. Nobody worked, neither on the dock nor on the boats. Carreia came down and shouted and swore, but we just looked at him without moving. At about 4:30 in the afternoon several trucks of armed police arrived. First they sealed off the gate to the street, then they ordered us back to work. When no one obeyed, they began moving slowly down the pier, now packed with striking workers.

This old captain friend of mine, Ocante Atobo, was leaning against the wall of the office shed. When the line of police reached the spot where he was, an officer suddenly raised his gun and shot him point blank in the chest. Ocante collapsed in a pool of blood. For a split second everyone froze - it was as if time stood still. Then hell broke loose. The police moved down the pier, shooting like crazy into the crowd. Men were screaming and running in all directions. I was over by my cousin Augusto Fernandes' boat, the 'Alio Sulemane.' Augusto, who was standing next to me, had his chest shot wide open; it was like his whole inside was coming out. He was crying: 'Oh God, Joao kill me, please.' But it wasn't necessary; when I lifted his head from the ground he was already dead.

Now the men were running for the end of the pier. The tide was out so all the boats and *pirogues* (African canoes) were resting on the beach. To hide there, however, was impossible since the police, standing high up on the dock, were shooting right into them. One officer was kneeling on the edge, firing at those trying to get away in the water. All around me people were shouting, 'Run, run!' but I stayed beside my dead cousin. 'No, if they want to kill me, let them do it right here.'

I don't know how long this had lasted when a PIDE inspector named Emmanuel Correia arrived and ordered the firing to stop. The last one to die was a boatman hiding in the mud under his *pirogue*, out of sight of the police. A Portuguese merchant, however, spotted him from his apartment window and shot him in the back with his hunting rifle just after Correia had arrived. One Portuguese, Romeo Martins, always a friend of the Africans, had been trying to keep the police from shooting, but all by himself he couldn't do much.

When the massacre finally ended I saw dead and wounded men all over: on the dock, on the beach, in the boats, in the water - everywhere. Among the dead were Caesare Fernandes and Jose de Pina who had worked for the Party. Afterwards we were taken to the police for interrogation. For three straight days I had to report to the administrator, Guerra Ribeiro, who wanted to know who had organized the strike. My answer was always the same: 'We all organized it; our wages are so bad we had no choice.' Later, when Ribeiro had finished his inquiry, the wage went up to 14 escudos a day.

Soon after the massacre a message from Amilcar Cabral was secretly circulated among us. It said that 3 August would never be forgotten and that we now had to organize to win our independence from Portuguese colonialism. Since then we never looked back. Many other workers and I joined the Party and started the difficult work of political mobilization here in Bissau. With experience of Pidjiguiti behind us, we knew that we had to accept the risks and sacrifices of an armed revolution to win freedom for our people.

'We Don't Accept Being Treated Like Animals'

Caby na luk is a Tchugue homen grande *(elder) who worked with us to collect information on his people and the armed struggle in the Tombali region.*

I was born here in Tchugue more than 70 years ago and have lived here all my life. As a small boy I looked after the animals and when I got a little older, my father taught me to work in the fields. All the work was done in groups; together we cultivated the plots of each *moranca* in turn. After work we boys gathered for the *n'gnae,* the old Balanta dances, like our ancestors had done before us. It was only when the war began that these traditions started to disappear.

My father was the one who told me how to live like a Balanta. He said that a man must learn to work hard early in his life, he must never steal from the other villagers or insult anybody. He taught me how to fight with sticks to defend myself, but told me never to use knives or other dangerous weapons. 'This is how my people always lived and this is how you shall live too,' he said.

When my father was a boy, there were no Whites in Tchugue. His father had told him about a white tribe living somewhere in Guine but it was only when my father was older that the Portuguese arrived in our *tabanca.* They had many weapons. In other villages where our people resisted, the Whites brought in Fula and Mandinga with guns and since we Balanta had nothing but sticks and swords, there was little we could do.

We continued to work hard but never got rich. How could we when the Portuguese never paid us the value of our work? For a huge basket of rice we were paid only 15 escudos (about 60 cents). This is why we grew up to hate the merchants: we never saw the fruits of our labor.

Later the Portuguese started forcing us to work on the roads.

They came and gathered all the men and took us far away. We worked hard from sun-up to sun-down and weren't even allowed to stop for a drink of water. When the food we had brought was finished, we had to find things to eat in the bush at night. So for many days we ate almost nothing. And they would beat us for the smallest thing, with sticks, whips or the *palmatoria.* *

We paid all kinds of taxes: on people, huts, animals and even bicycles. At my father's death I slaughtered ten cows in his homage. When the Portuguese found out, they demanded 1,000 escudos in taxes, 100 for each cow. I tell you, they took everything we had!

The *tugas* appointed a Balanta 'chief' in our village, Fuab na Digna. This Fuab made us all suffer. Whenever someone built up a small herd of cattle, he would confiscate it or have the person pay extra taxes to him personally. He made people work in his fields for no pay and took rice from the plots of others. When we complained to the Portuguese administrator, he told us to shut up and go home. Fuab was also the only one in Tchugue who had a rifle for hunting in the forest.

We all got very tired of this Portuguese colonialism. Our god put us here on earth so we could at least have something, to live together in friendship and cooperation. But how can we tolerate somebody who treats us as the colonialists did? We don't accept being treated like animals, beaten and killed for nothing. That is why we united in the Party to put an end to colonialism.

One night Nino came to my *moranca* and told me about a party which was preparing a war to chase the Portuguese from Guine. He said there was no place in our country where the people could live in peace and prosperity and that we had to save our children from this system. I knew he was right, that we had to resist. The life of one person is nothing for the freedom of a whole people. I was the first one in our region to know and I only told a few trusted people about it. In other *tabancas* the Portuguese got to know and killed many people.

My people suffered much in the war. When the Party attacked Tchugue, the *tugas* destroyed everything before they left. Later, the planes and helicopters killed and destroyed even more. But when the *tugas* later returned with many troops and installed themselves, I refused to flee. I said to myself: 'They may kill me, but I will stay and look after my things, I'm too old to start again with nothing.' Life became very difficult with the Portuguese back. For example, one day they took my best cow and when I went to get it

---

* A wooden paddle with conical holes drilled in it. When hit with a *palmatoria,* skin and tissue are drawn up into the narrowing holes. If hit hard and often enough, the skin will break.

back, they killed it right before my eyes and insulted me before they let me go home. I hope I will never again have to go through things like that.

Now the time has finally arrived when we can live in peace and enjoy the products of our work. In my *moranca* we are building new huts to house all my children and grandchildren. Later we will join with the others in reconstructing the whole village to make it a good place for the young people to grow up.

Whoever comes to my people as a friend is received as one. The Portuguese took advantage of our friendship to exploit us, so we had to chase them back to Portugal. For a long time we believed that they were the only white tribe in the world. Colonialism closed our eyes to the world around us. But now the Party has changed this and when we meet people like you - from a far away country and who work with our Party - we shall do all we can to help you in your work. It is a pleasure for me to tell you about my life and the war in our village. And I will gladly do the same for any other friend from abroad who comes with the same mission.

Women in the Struggle: Liberation Is a Process

From a slave-like existence under colonialism and archaic social structures, many of Guinea-Bissau's women have become leading cadres of the PAIGC and today set an example for their sisters as thousands of women are moving beyond their traditional roles. Chantal Sarrazin drew from her experiences with Guinean women inspiration to develop her own confidence and abilities as a political person.

Everywhere, I saw women with infants strapped to their backs, preparing meals, working in the fields; women who were doing the chores that have always been their lot in an agricultural, male-dominated society.

But this initial impression only takes a short while to be replaced by a different appraisal once I really start investigating the gains made by the women of Guinea-Bissau since the beginning of the national liberation struggle. Certainly, things have not been turned completely upside-down in relation to the past, but neither had I expected them to be so. It is only while working in day-to-day contact with the people, however, that I come to realize the depth of the changes that have taken place.

One of the first women I got to know was Cidu na Quida, a 55-year-old woman from Tchugue village. When PAIGC militants first came to clandestinely organize in her village, Cidu was the first woman to be informed. At that time, those who worked with the Party had to be very secretive since there were traitors among the population. The traditional idea that women could not keep secrets was still in force, but Cidu's husband trusted and confided in her.

At first, Cidu prepared food at home for the embryonic guerrilla units in the forest. But soon the war engulfed the entire southern part of the country, and the villagers, too, had to evacuate to the forest. From that time until the end of the war, Cidu worked as a cook in one of PAIGC's military bases.

Before the war started, she had persuaded her youngest son, Manuel, to join the guerrillas. This was no easy task. He had been sent to study at a mission school, but when the Party began mobilizing for the struggle, Cidu changed her mind about the boy's future. She walked many days to the school to talk to her son, only to find that the priests had done their work well: Manuel wanted nothing to do with the 'bandits.' Cidu, however, insisted. 'You must help us liberate ourselves from the Portuguese. We must stop being treated like slaves.'

It was unusual for a woman to express such political concerns so his mother's words impressed Manuel very much. Soon after, he ran away from the school and joined the liberation movement. After some years of service in the swampy southern forests and further military training in the Soviet Union, he became a FARP commander in the North.

Cidu's actions showed her strong commitment and dedication to the struggle. She encouraged her husband to work for the PAIGC and she demanded that her sons join the guerrillas though this could mean death or, at a minimum, long periods of separation. Her eldest son, Bedan Santa, who became the leader of the Tchugue village militia, suffered three years of imprisonment and torture after being captured by the Portuguese. Another son was killed by the colonial air force, and her husband died in the difficult years in the forest. The pain still shows in her face when she speaks of her experiences.

When I was not otherwise busy I wandered around the village to visit people and to capture their daily life with my camera. At times some of the younger women took me along to pick green mangos which we ate with a pinch of salt. Our communication was through a hand sign language by which we managed to say a great deal. A favorite preoccupation of theirs was to play with my short straight hair and try to make braids hold in it.

I was always impressed with the physical strength and skills of the women around me. They take charge of all domestic work and participate in all stages of rice production. Because of the primitive cultivation techniques, eight months of the year is devoted to the annual crop. Fortunately our visit coincided with the end of the dry season, the one period when there is relatively little to do. But the women are still busy. An hour before the sun is up, their pounding of rice fills the *tabanca* with a rhythmic, thudding sound. The morning meal takes about two hours to prepare and afterwards they gather at the well to wash clothes or fetch water in huge clay jars. Later, after more food preparation and the midday break some walk to the far fields to husk the remainder of last year's rice crop. This is done by vigorously beating bundles of dried rice plants with a t-shaped stick until all the grain has fallen off. Most of the sixty-pound baskets they carry home will be taken to the People's Store and sold.

Back home it is time to pound rice for the evening meal, again bending over the mortar. It looked quite simple until I tried it myself and found that the force of the whole body must be used in hitting the exact center of the mortar, slightly turning the pestle with each stroke. The young girl who tried to teach me had many a good laugh as the mortar bounced around and the rice scattered on the ground.

Colonialism had no interest in helping the Guine villagers to adopt new and easier production techniques. Labor power was extremely cheap for the administrators and merchants who exploited the wealth produced by Cidu and the others. But now the people can move forward from this colonially retarded state. The introduction of technology as basic as running water, for example, will qualitatively change the condition of women, releasing energy to develop themselves and their country.

After leaving Tchugue, we spent a week recording the life story of Dalme M'Bunde, one of the FARP militants who served as our guard and translator during our entire stay in the South. Dalme knew this region very well from his ten years of fighting in the bush, and was anxious to share his experiences. Now that the war was over, his family had found him a wife - a girl he vaguely remembered having played with at his home village many years ago. He was proud to make the announcement; as a married man he would get a separate hut and an extra monthly allowance from the army.

It surprised me at first that a politically conscious militant like Dalme would agree to have his wife chosen for him by his parents and vice versa. After all, the Party had initiated a campaign against forced marriage, polygamy and the bride-price system at the outset of the struggle. Was this marriage not a sign of political retrogression?

I no longer think the answer is so simple. The revolution cannot change all aspects of negative traditions overnight. First, the worst customs have to be eliminated - forced marriage is in fact already illegal. Other measures are being designed to do away with polygamy without causing economic hardship for those women who completely depend on their husbands for their subsistence. Polygamy is no longer practiced by Party militants. Dalme and his wife were both happy with the arrangement. The marriage was neither forced, nor polygamous; it was therefore consistent with PAIGC principles. Still, that the relationship was not initiated by the two young people themselves shows there is some distance to go in transforming Guine society.

Though some customs, like polygamy, are practiced among all the ethnic groups of Guinea-Bissau, there are also great differences between the traditions of the various groups. In more equitable societies, like that of the Balantes of Tchugue, women labor in the fields and at home while the men, too, work in the fields when they are not hunting, fishing, or constructing new huts. It was not so among the islamized tribes of the North and East, the Fula and Mandinga, where in the past rigid social and religious structures left women both with the major productive role and in complete subordination to their husbands and the male village hierarchy.

But here, too, things are changing, as I find out during my stay in the Mandinga village of Mores. This village became famous as the center of fighting during the liberation war and was completely destroyed by Portuguese bombs and artillery. Only a few burnt sticks mark the former location of huts, and the people are now rebuilding everything. Naturally, the problems are many: shortage of food and shelter for the refugees returning every day from Senegal, inadequate diet, epidemics, and an incredibly high infant mortality rate. The Government is trying to help out with seeds, grain, and other foods to last until the next harvest. A small hospital, a power plant, a school, and, for the first time, an ample water supply, now make Mores a better place to live than before. In these surroundings I recorded the life story of Binta Seidi.

As Binta told her story, I began to grasp the depth of Mandinga women's oppression. She is probably in her late sixties (there are no written birth records) and has known brutally hard labor all her life. Every year, after the rains had washed away the roads, the Portuguese forced the villagers to rebuild them. Only the small children and the very old went free. For several months every year Binta left home by four in the morning to be at work by daybreak. Together with the others she was beaten and not even allowed to sit down and eat the food she brought for the day. Many fainted and some died under the unbearable heat of the midday sun. They worked until dark. The Portuguese made them work 'until you can no longer see your own skin.'

Men, too, had to work on the roads. Within the village, however, their life was one of relative leisure. For instance, the men would plant the cotton while the women's tasks were to prepare the fields, weed, pick, and spin before the men concluded the process by weaving. While the women usually worked all day, men often found time to sit around and discuss village affairs.

Then the liberation war started. Under the influence of the PAIGC, the men started to work harder to produce enough food for the fighters, and many joined the guerrilla army. The Party cadres had to struggle with the village leaders, and the pressure of the war helped forge some change. Today, even though the situation has improved, I still see groups of men lounging in the shade while their wives and daughters work.

Binta responded to PAIGC's call by bringing food to the guerrillas in the forest, always risking capture by the Portuguese forces. She also cared for her aging husband and was soon elected to serve on the village committee - a tremendous responsibility for a woman in Mandinga society. As a leader in her village Binta was forced to cope with the timidity and internalized sense of inferiority that is the heritage of women in most male-dominated societies.

A similar transition also took place in our personal relationship. Having met no Whites but the Portuguese colonialists, Binta was at first afraid to come to my hut by herself. But soon we became quite close, and I often paid visits to her family's huts on the eastern fringe of the village. One day, near the end of our work, she arrived with some rice wrapped in a piece of cloth. 'Do you have a mother where you come from?' she asked me. 'Tell her to pound this rice for you. And tell her that you now have another mother here in Guine.'

Binta's strength and enthusiasm were infectious. With the war over, and the end of her own life probably not too far off, she was still planning for the future. Working with her filled me with a deep optimism for the future of our common struggle. Seeing how she and I, two women of vastly different backgrounds could work together as comrades, has given me new strength and inspiration for my own political activities.

Cidu and Binta are among the village women who, through the initiation of PAIGC, set the trend for greater and greater participation by women as the liberation struggle developed. They were not satisfied to merely watch their husbands and sons do political and military work. At first their contributions were extensions of women's traditional spheres of work, growing food and cooking for the guerrillas. Later they took on greater responsibilities. They helped transport war supplies and worked as nurses with the combat units or in the liberated areas behind the fighting lines. Few became part of the regular army although many participated in local militias. Many proved extremely capable in mobilizing the population and were made political commissars or elected to village committees and the

People's Tribunals.

PAIGC helped women to confront tribal traditions and deep-rooted prejudice to demonstrate that without the participation of women the liberation of the country could not be achieved. For women like Cidu and Binta, this struggle was essential in breaking down the widespread resistance to the advancement of women. It also helped release the energy of thousands of younger women - their daughters, nieces, and granddaughters - for still new areas of involvement.

Most of my Guinean women friends belong to this new generation. Ana Maria Gomes, for instance, was sent by her mother, who headed the local village committee, to join the liberation movement when she was thirteen. In the PAIGC camps she learned to read and write and received basic military training. Later she studied nursing in the USSR and became one of the Party's leading medical workers in the North. Her training abroad helped give her a wider perspective on the aims of the liberation struggle; her village background provided work discipline and a strong sense of responsibility. As an enthusiastic teacher of hygiene and preventive medicine to the population, she was made a political commissar at twenty and later elected to represent the Sara region of the People's National Assembly. Other friends, like Josefina and Sadjo, have similar stories to tell. Both joined PAIGC as young girls and were later sent to Cuba for training, Sadjo as a nurse, Fina as a filmmaker.

Before beginning my work in Guinea-Bissau, I didn't fully appreciate how the armed struggle was just a step in a longer revolutionary process. Neither did I realize what tremendous sacrifices lay behind the changes taking place - sacrifices in human lives, in separation from families, and in endless hard work. Their history has taught the people of Guine that the progress in their lives can only come through continuous hard work and struggle on their own part.

Guinean women have already made considerable progress. The students, in particular, make great efforts to change cultural roles; boys take on domestic tasks at school, girls help construct huts. Both women and men are being trained as nurses and teachers.

Yet many contradictions remain and long struggles lie ahead; it is still too soon to see how far and how fast women will move beyond their traditional spheres of work. During a visit to the nursing school in Mores, for instance, I observed that the women students had special problems. Under the colonial system very few women were educated while many of the male students here have had some previous schooling. Consequently, the women were not as fluent in Portuguese and had more difficulties with their studies. The female political commissar of the group felt that the women also had the added burden of inferiority complexes and needed special support for their efforts. Also, with the needs of the armed struggle no longer imposing themselves, the pressure of traditions now reasserts itself. Marriage with child rearing and domestic responsibilities weighs heavily on many of the women cadres who thus have to carry a double load.

Under the Portuguese, Guinea-Bissau stood still, its productive forces frozen. Then, the armed struggle threw all aspects of society into motion. Necessity of war could legitimately bring into question the old ways of relating or doing things. This was the basis for change, but transforming the centuries-old role of women required PAIGC's leadership and conscious struggle. Today underdevelopment is the greatest obstacle to emancipating women. To go further, Guinean women must be freed from ignorance and superstition, have adequate medical care to plan families and avoid the waste of infant mortality, and be released from the drudgery of a marginal subsistence economy. But material development in itself is not a guarantee. The mobilization of women must continue to be a conscious element in the process to fully develop the potential of Guine's men and women.

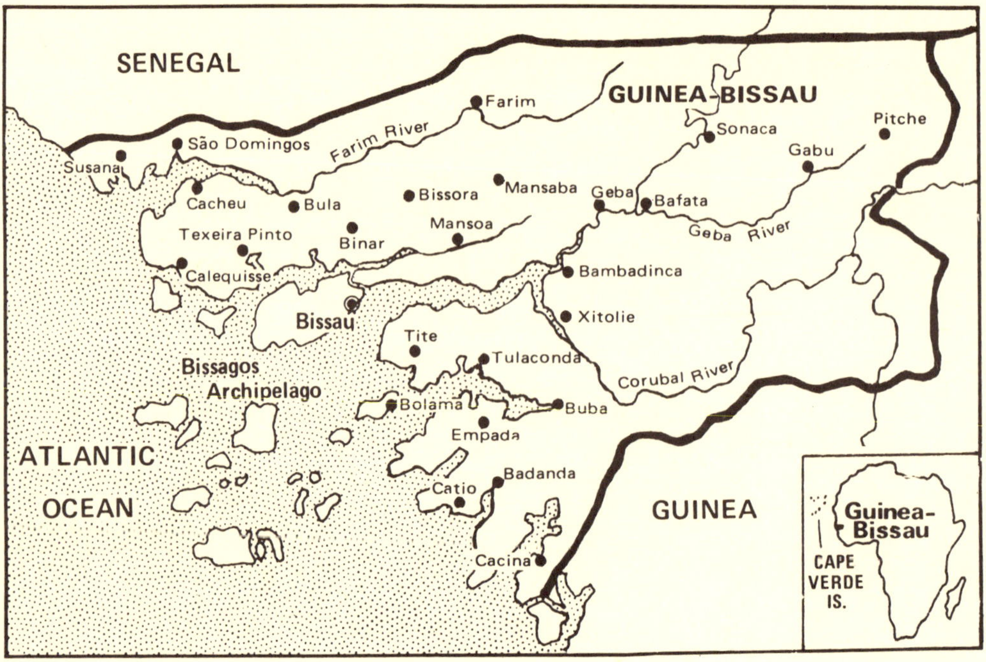

GUINEA-BISSAU covers 14,000 square miles and holds a population of approximately 900,000. The major ethnic groups are the Balanta, the Fula, the Mandinga, and the Mandjak. The coastal and southern parts of the country are well suited to rice cultivation, while the groundnuts, millet, corn, rice, and cattle are raised on the savannah plateaus of the interior. The south-eastern region also holds considerable bauxite deposits.

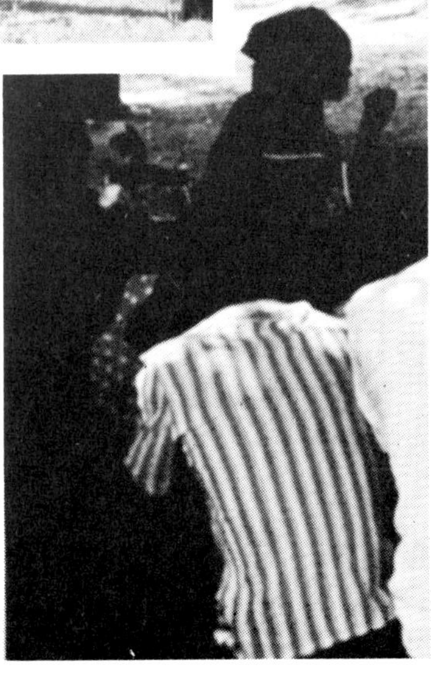

Left: 'From dawn to dusk the villagers labored to rebuild their huts before the rainy season.' p. 21

Below: In the shade of a Tchugue mango tree the villagers accepted us as comrades and agreed to cooperate in our work.

'The morning mist has not yet cleared when the women arrive, straight backs and knees slightly bent to absorb the body movement as they balance big baskets on their heads.' p. 67

Top: Two generations of women militants: Ana Maria Gomes and Binta Seidi meet at Mores.

Bottom: Palm nuts to be sold at Mores People's Store.

1

3

2

1) *Kau: like a fish in water*

2) *Cidu: a deep commitment*

3) *Caby: tired of being exploited*

4) *Da Costa: he survived the massacre*

5) *Binta: she worked hard all her life*

6) *Carmen: a forceful leader*

4

6

5

The People's Stores are more than places to buy things; they represent a means for the people to give their independence a material content.

Fidelis Almada, the Secretary of Justice: *'Our cadres have to struggle with the people; new laws have to be explained and discussed again and again. In this way the courts advance the people's political consciousness.' p. 84*

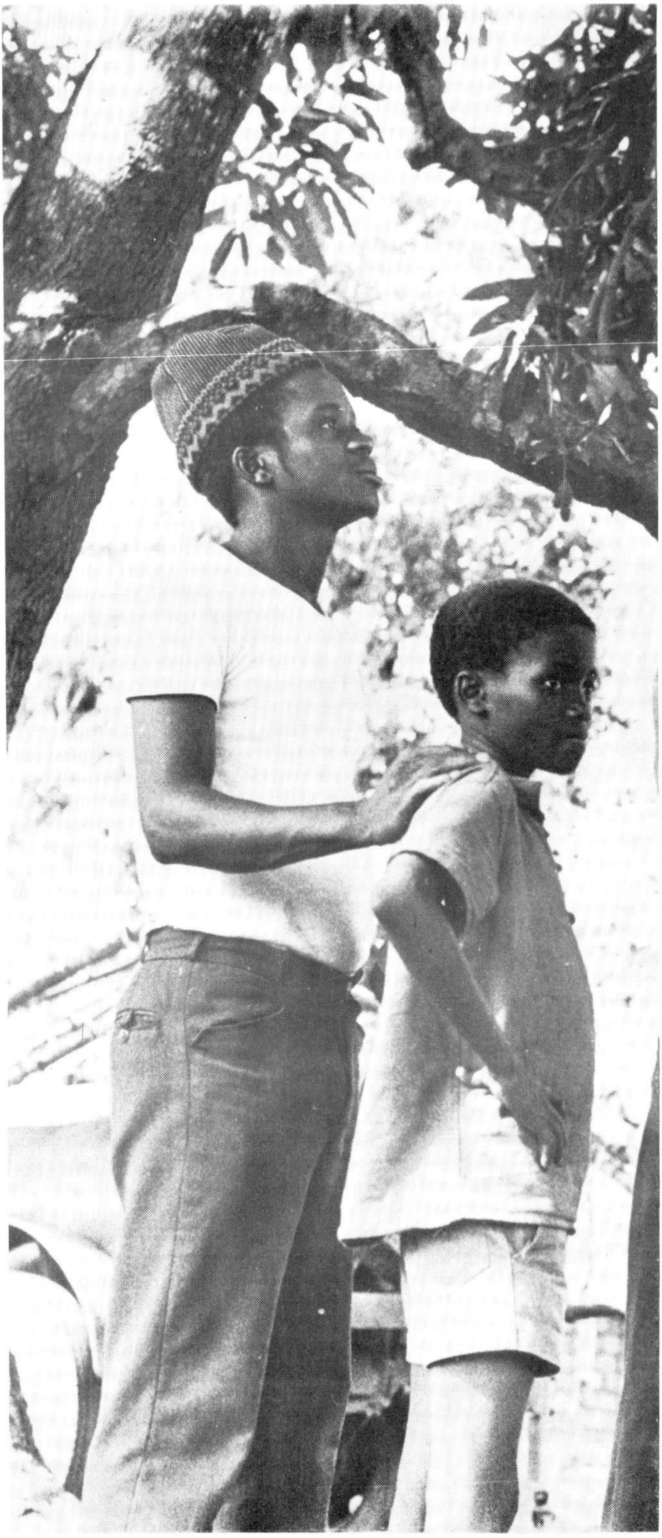

'Their schooling has been an integral part of the struggle; they have worked the land, carried supplies, and even taught those with less training then themselves. This is the essence of PAIGC's education philosophy: integrate book learning with the lives and culture of the people; mold cadres to serve the interests of the masses.' p. 89

Carmen Pereira: Woman Revolutionary

Carmen Pereira is one of the most dynamic and forceful leaders of the PAIGC. Today, as during the liberation war, people flock from afar to hear her speak at meetings throughout the country. With her many urgent responsibilities, we were fortunate to have the opportunity to discuss with her some of the questions around the involvement of women in the Guinea-Bissau revolution.

Comrade Pereira, can you briefly tell us how and why you joined the PAIGC?

I come from a family which was well-off by African standards and much respected in the city of Bissau. My father was one of the few African lawyers. But I saw what the Portuguese did in my country: wealth for a few, with extreme poverty for the great majority. I saw them putting my Guinean brothers and sisters in prison for the smallest protest, and I realized that this life was not a good one.

I first heard of PAIGC in 1961. Then, one day I discovered Party documents my husband was hiding; I told him he should have talked to me about the struggle. In 1962 the repression in the towns really escalated. My husband was in danger and decided to slip out of the country to join the Party abroad. I was on my own but soon began making my own plans to go and work for the Party. Later that year I managed to get out of Bissau with my two children and baby. On the way we passed by a concentration camp in Tite and saw prisoners being treated very badly by the Portuguese. Some had been so badly tortured they were bloody and lying on the ground, unable to get up. This confirmed my decision to go and join the Party.

In Senegal I met Amilcar Cabral, who encouraged me. But I had myself and the children to support, so I went to Zinguinchor on the border of Guinea-Bissau where I worked as a seamstress. From my wages I was able to feed my children and 30 Party comrades at the same time. I was 25 years old and my political understanding was just starting to develop.

What responsibilities have you had since then?

At the end of 1963 I was sent for political and nursing training in the Soviet Union. After 11 months abroad I returned to carry on the function I had at the border. The armed struggle had been launched and soon the Party gave me another responsibility: finding safe places for treating our casualties, and then teaching nursing to a group of young women. Later, I was sent to the South Front as a health *responsavel* (cadre) and opened the first Party hospital in our country. At first it was difficult to convince the population to come to the hospital for treatment. Under the colonialists one had to pay to receive treatment, so the people were not accustomed to doctors and nurses. The Party organized health brigades to give medicines to the population and teach them modern hygiene and the importance of seeing a doctor.

At the end of 1967, the Party appointed me political commissar of all the South Front. At that time many people thought a woman couldn't carry out a responsibility like that. My work required a lot of travelling, and walking was the only way. Many ambushes were set up by the colonialists. I was responsible for the political mobilization of all people - men and women - in that region. I put my children in Party schools and committed myself completely to the political work.

In 1969 I was appointed member of the Executive Committee of the Struggle. That same year I was given responsibility for the national reconstruction of the South Front. It was hard work. One had to oversee the operation of all sanitary posts and other facilities. In 1973 we had our first session of the National Assembly. The enemy tried desperately to prevent it: they sent planes to drop bombs and massacre the population, hoping to stop the deputies from meeting. Despite this we had our Assembly; it was a great accomplishment. I was elected as deputy for Bissau, Vice-President for the National Assembly and member of the State Council. After this Assembly - at which we made our formal declaration of independence - I returned to the South Front. I told the population how we'd managed to hold the Assembly and what decisions were taken. I explained everything to them because they were the ones who fought to make the National Assembly possible.

After the fall of colonialism, I came here to Bissau. I am now working for the Secretariat-General as a member of the Party's Executive Committee of Struggle and the Commission of Organization at the national level.

As a woman revolutionary, what problems have you had and how have you been able to deal with them?

Before I joined the struggle I was very timid and didn't speak much. I couldn't be among people too long because I was shy. And I was very afraid when seeing people with guns. Now, I don't hesitate to talk and have learned to use a gun myself. This change is due in large part to the advice of our great comrade Amilcar Cabral. His writings, the seminars he gave us and the many conversations we had with him were a tremendous inspiration and gave me the confidence to struggle.

I have learned that the first thing one must have is political determination. To win the people's respect and confidence it is necessary to be disciplined and serious about one's responsibilities. It is especially important to follow every directive and line of the Party. With the people's respect and confidence one can work without too many difficulties.

What was the woman's position in the traditional system of Guinea-Bissau?

There are many tribes and each one has its own customs. Among the Muslim tribes the position of women was very backward. To greet her husband, for example, a woman would have to kneel and put her forehead on the floor. She went to work and the husband stayed home. She worked till sundown, came home, greeted her husband, prepared the meal, got some water for him to wash with, brought him food and knelt before giving it to him. The Party has struggled against such negative traditions and done away with most of that. Now men work with the women in the fields.

In the past a Muslim man never wanted a woman to go to a meeting. There were many meetings during the struggle and women were very interested to hear what was going on. The men would refuse to let them go for three or four times, but the women would keep insisting. Finally, the men were obliged to accept. Now, women are on the village committees and are sometimes elected president. Men now accept women leading meetings because it is a Party directive and they see why it is correct.

But there is still work to be done. After our coming to Bissau, the President of the State Committee in Gabu had many problems with the Fula tribesmen. They could accept anything except having women on their village committee. So we did some political work. To inaugurate a house just built in Gabu, President Lay-Sec invited me. He called a meeting for the population and I led it. At first, men were upset to see a woman leading, but afterwards they were satisfied. Ever since that day, they have let women participate in meetings and committees.

There are, of course, still problems with backward traditions. The

Party's approach is to struggle against what goes counter to our principles and particular goals at each stage of the struggle. We can't change these traditions overnight. Only the evolution of the struggle will overcome all the negative aspects of tradition.

What is the situation regarding polygamy? What is the Party doing to overcome it?

Polygamy, in a country which has been backward for so long, is very difficult to combat. In the countryside it is still common because of the traditional economic structure. Polygamy is not illegal yet and the Party has not taken any severe measures against it. But we are doing much political work to show that it is no longer necessary, especially in the cities. In meetings we talk about the negative aspects of polygamy; Party militants can only have monogamous marriages; women can now get divorces; and our youth are growing up believing in monogamy because of the new education. Little by little we will overcome polygamy.

How did women participate in the armed struggle?

From the beginning women played an active and essential part in gaining the independence of our country. Throughout the struggle we did vital clandestine work. Men, having to carry identification cards, couldn't do this work as well. We brought food to the guerrillas. Also, the Local Armed Forces (FAL) included women, some of whom became commanders. Many women became nurses, trained by the Party either abroad or inside the country. And all nurses received military training. They had to be military people as well as nurses so they could defend their patients and themselves if attacked by the enemy. Other women, in addition to their regular functions, became political commissars. In all areas of the struggle women's participation was vital to our success.

Some nurses trained by the Party left their responsibilities after they got married and had some children. How did you deal with that problem? Does it still exist?

Yes, during the armed struggle we did have some problems like that. Everyone has his or her own problems in life, and some individuals put these ahead of the interests of the Party. Some nurses returned from abroad and wanted to spend their time just treating their sick parents; others abandoned their posts and went to where their husbands were. We had to struggle a lot with this problem, to educate these militants about the necessity of carrying out one's responsibility and serving the whole people. Generally, this education work was quite effective.

National reconstruction, like the armed struggle, demands certain sacrifices - for example, the separation of couples. Some nurses I met accepted this by saying: 'I do what the Party wants.' Considering women's traditional role of subordination, do you think there is a danger of their accepting directives without understanding why?

We are in a crucial stage in Guinea-Bissau: we need to defend our independence, and begin improving the material conditions of the people. For example, there are still traitors and enemies in the country; our army needs to be ready in both the towns and countryside. And health conditions are very bad in the countryside; we need to send our nurses to sanitation clinics throughout the country. Sometimes this means that couples need to be separated so as to carry out responsibilities in different geographic areas. The Party and State are doing much to bring couples together, but sometimes separation is still necessary.

Our people understand that there is a great difference between the Party's authority and the old Portuguese colonialist authority. The Portuguese colonialists didn't give us time to see and learn and think; they were only interested in exploiting us. Now, under the Party, we have the chance of learning and developing. We are free. The nurses are free to say what they think; if there is some problem with their work they can discuss it with a responsible person in the Party.

The Party taught us the rights of women in our country. The Party led the liberation war, built the National Assembly, gave us the correct political orientation...the Party did everything. This is why young people respect what the Party says, and why the young nurses you talked with accept being separated from their husbands.

In some meetings I have noticed a timidity among the women to express their thoughts. How do you deal with this problem?

One thing we must do is reinforce the political brigades doing education work with such women, to continue to help them become politically stronger. Each work area, such as a hospital or production center, has regular meetings of all the people working there to discuss problems, raise criticisms, and so forth. At these political meetings sometimes the women don't dare get up and say what they are thinking. We are explaining to them why it is necessary for them to express their feelings, to speak out. Some of the women, mainly those who never lived in the liberated regions, are not used to meetings and so they are naturally timid. But we are going to keep reminding them to express themselves and, little by little, they will overcome this problem.

During the second session of the National Assembly this year, some people proposed that women pay taxes, as the men do. What is your opinion on this question?

These discussions were quite important. Some people thought that the women would get more autonomy by having to pay independent taxes. My opinion is that we need to distinguish between women in the towns and women in the countryside. In the countryside, a woman works with her husband and the product of their labor is for both, or for all, if it is polygamous. It would be very difficult for the peasant women to have to divide up their produce, figure out their taxes, and so forth. At this stage, it would only create more problems for them.

It is different in the towns and cities. Here, the women receive their own salary and can pay taxes. For example, at the end of the month I get a salary and I pay taxes; and the same for my husband. Once we have developed the countryside - improved the social and economic conditions, acquired machinery, established factories, etc. - then women there will be able to pay taxes too.

During the struggle the PAIGC did not form a special organization for women as other liberation movements did. Why?

At the beginning of the struggle the Party created the 'Democratic Union of Women of Guinea,' but we lacked cadre for this. All the experienced women were at the front - participating in the armed struggle, doing political work, etc.- so they could not take part in the organization.

Now that the war is over the Party has created a committee composed of ten leaders, cadres and militants of the Party. The committee is now preparing to organize the women of the Party. Last month we had a meeting and made a proposal to the Party about the type of women's organization we wish to have. As I am a member of the Executive Committee of the Party, this will pass through my hands. Soon we will be establishing our women's organization.

In the liberated zones the women know what a women's organization is and they are very interested in it. But in the zones formerly occupied by the enemy the women do not fully understand. So we will be doing more work to convince them of the importance of a women's organization. Political education...always.

The Struggle for the Primary Necessity

The system of People's Stores became a pillar of the new life in PAIGC's liberated regions during the war. Their present expansion throughout the country has now sharpened the class struggle.....

The morning mist has not yet cleared when the women start arriving in small groups, with straight backs and knees slightly bent to absorb body movement as they balance big baskets of rice on their heads, down the uneven village trails. Their loads are heavy; though the soothing morning breeze still fills the air, small streams of sweat form in the furrows of their necks and between their breasts as they help each other unload near the scales. Then they sit down to nurse the youngest, strapped on the back, or simply relax.

We are at the People's Store - the *armazen do povo* - in a small southern village. Temporarily located in a former Portuguese army hut, it has become a strong link between the villagers and the outside world and a focal point of village life since it was set up six months ago. This is especially true now in the trading season. The single Portuguese merchant who literally ruled here before the war, had his shop destroyed in a PAIGC attack and never returned.

At seven thirty sharp the two young cadres in charge of the store arrive and business can begin. The baskets are weighed and the rice emptied into a mounting heap in the granary - sixty-five, seventy, and even up to seventy-five pounds of unhulled rice in each. At a price of about six cents a pound this is the average Tombali family's only steady source of cash. The figures are noted in a big book and payment takes place on the spot. Each woman wraps her money in a small piece of cloth which is then closed with a solid knot and carefully tucked into the brightly-colored waistcloth worn by all Balanta women. Those who need something for the day disappear into the store while the others head straight back to the *moranca.* Before the sun gets too hot, they'll be out in the fields again for tomorrow's basketful, babies on their backs, as always.

Inside, on unfinished shelves or in orderly piles on the hard-packed earthen floor, is a selection of the 'primary necessities' carried by all People's Stores: sugar, flour, cooking oil, cloth, soap, tobacco, matches, lanterns and aluminum kitchenware. The counter is made up of long sticks placed over two empty oil drums. A set-up rough by any standard, but it won't stay like this for long explains the comrade in charge: the villagers have started collective construction of a new building which they hope will be ready for the rainy season. Right now, however, they are waiting for more materials to arrive from Bissau, by the same boat which will take their rice to the capital for later distribution in other parts of the country.

From Tombali to Gabu, from Boe to Canchungo a network of People's Stores now assures an adequate supply of basic goods. The produce exchanged varies with the regions; rice in the South, peanuts, palm products and hides from the North and East. Already at an early stage in the liberation struggle the People's Stores became a cornerstone of life in the liberated areas - a small taste of the future to indicate what could be done later when conditions improved. By paying the peasants more for their products and selling its own merchandise for less than did the Portuguese, the PAIGC at once gave the people a material incentive to stay in the liberated zones and broke the monopoly of the colonial trading companies. Although suffering from problems of supply and Portuguese air attacks, the system expanded steadily as the liberation movement gained control over more and more of the national territory. The end of the armed struggle and proclamation of independence have in no way lessened the stores' importance. In Güinea-Bissau colonialism rested on a system of forced exchange - the peasants were made to grow certain crops useful to the colonial economy - and the entire commercial structure was developed exclusively to enhance this process. Faced with such a heritage and the unwillingness of many merchants to adapt to the new reality, the immediate objective of the *armazens* is to supply primary necessities to the population throughout the country while putting an end to speculation and black-marketing, in itself no small task to start with. Their long-term aim, a distribution system to serve the interests of the popular masses, makes them a key tool in the struggle to build a new Guine. 'Let us use our stores as a weapon,' says an editorial in the semi-official *No Pintcha* newspaper, 'not to kill people, but to kill the unbridled exploitation of man by man, a heritage of colonial domination.'

As in all other spheres of the national reconstruction process, the struggle for the People's Stores is essentially political, a battle of the new against the old, of socialism against primitive mercantile capitalism. But again, regional variations are great. The war virtually eliminated the colonial system in large parts of the rural areas; only within the perimeters of the fortified Portuguese posts could the merchants find relative safety while their profit-shed was being increasingly curtailed by the expanding liberated zones. True, they may have enjoyed a more or less captive audience in the surrounding strategic villages, but as the army prohibited the population to work in the fields from fear that they would escape, there was not much to be traded. The basis of colonial commerce was therefore gradually eroded. Add to this the destruction of dozens of stores during military operations and its backruptcy is virtually total as far as the countyside is concerned. Toward the end of the war, for instance, exports could cover no more than ten per cent of Guine's annual budget. Today the People's Stores are the only outlets for imported goods in the old liberated areas while in the former Portuguese-held posts they have been introduced as an alternative to those private merchants who have chosen to remain.

In the towns, and particularly in Bissau, the situation is far more complex. Some Portuguese merchants returned to their homeland before the final colonial departure to escape the 'Communist takeover.' The majority, however, decided to stay - at least for the time being - to see what would develop. Not altogether incorrectly, they calculated that, together with the few African and Lebanese traders, their services would remain indispensable for some time to come and, after all, people of their class have been riding similar storms in other places, in one way or another.

Riding the storm, yes, but many had even greater ambitions. First they sent most of their wealth out of the country. Then, in the wake of the Portuguese departure, with the new regime reorganizing the administrative apparatus and much political uncertainty in the capital, a torrent of price increases suddenly hit the population. Soon after, essential goods, notably rice and cooking oil, started to disappear from the shelves. A first sign of the failure of independence? 'We told you so,' was the tune from the lower part of town where the merchant houses lie huddled at the base of the old Portuguese citadel, antique cannon muzzles assuringly pointing over their rooftops. 'What did you expect?'

But this brought things into the open and the Government reacted quickly. 'We know that certain persons continue to exploit our people,' thundered Chico Mendes, Prime Minister and one of the four members of PAIGC's Permanent Secretariat, in a broadcasted speech. 'The merchants of Bissau are doing so, manipulating prices and hoarding goods while saying that the PAIGC is to blame. Today they want ten escudos, tomorrow fifteen, and when you ask them why, they tell you, 'Don't blame me; it's the PAIGC's fault.' We know this type of merchant all too well and have no confidence in them when it comes to the reconstruction of our country. All they can think about is how to fill their bellies and purses!' In an emergency move food prices were frozen and strict marketing rules imposed, including severe penalties for concealing merchandise.

The next step was to set up a price control commission with powers to enforce its decisions. Now, offenders will get no easy breaks, promises Armando Ramos, Minister of Commerce and Crafts. The commission 'will propose laws to discipline economic activity and be able to suppress all violators. It will exercise economic as well as political sanctions and will at regular intervals determine the prices of primary necessities. Hopefully, the commission can start its work very soon so as to enable us to detect and severely punish all offenders.'

These are defensive measures, efforts to control and remold old structures to fit new realities, but they have still proven quite effective in checking these first counter-revolutionary abuses by the small Bissau bourgeoisie. To turn the tide, however, to seize the strategic offensive and secure the advance of the revolution against the resistance of such elements, a more basic and constructive program is needed. The Government's strongest card here is no doubt the system of People's Stores which has now been expanded to cover the entire country, operating at import/export, wholesale and retail levels. Already more than twenty temporary outlets have been set up in the Bissau *bairros* alone where they have monopolized the sale of primary necessities to prevent a repetition of the past. Like the other *armazens*, they are run by employees of the People's Store state corporation but in close coordination with the Party's *bairro* committees. As in the villages, the rough sheds, huts or old storage rooms which locate the shops for the time being, are more than simply places to buy things; they represent a means for the population to free themselves from the grip of the past and take some steps to flesh out the skeletal framework that formal independence has provided.

This may sound a little far-fetched to the average North American, daily confronted with almighty food corporations and their nightmarish super-dumps. But to the large majority of Bissau's *bairro* population, always uncomfortably close to that invisible hunger line, the thought of not only getting food cheaper, but also being able to have a say in what goods the store should stock, opens new horizons. Thus we see long queues and endless discussions about the pros and cons of a particular item at *bairro* committee meetings. The *armazens* have clearly become a crucial factor in the mobilization of this population in the struggle to dress the still nearly naked frame of people's power and block the path of those who merely want to wrap the old frame in new clothing. 'Our task is clear,' says Justino Santos

Nunes, Vice President of the Belem and Missira *bairro* committee, confidently. 'The people in our *bairro* are certainly interested in securing their elementary needs. But they are also conscious of the stores' political significance and are vigilant and alert when it comes to using them against the speculation of the bourgeois opportunists.' Clearly, the ideas of a new Guine are beginning to sprout even in this neighborhood where only a few years ago Spinola managed to recruit many African mercenaries.

In October 1964 a column of 68 PAIGC guerrillas and carriers crossed the border from the Republic of Guinea loaded with supplies for the first People's Store. Their trail was both difficult and dangerous with rivers to cross and days of marching through heavy fighting areas. A few days from the border the group was ambushed by a Portuguese unit but managed to salvage the supplies and get them safely to their destination in the Cubisseco zone. In November that year the stores began operating.

Eleven years later the picture is vastly different. Goods now arrive by ship to Bissau where they are sorted and stored at the main depot, a former Portuguese army installation whose ten warehouses are already growing too small for the operation's needs. One shed alone is filled with sugar from Cuba and the USSR, another with Portuguese cement and a third with Argentinian rice. Though Guinea-Bissau used to export a large part of its 80,000 tons annual pre-war crops, more than half of its current 30,000 ton minimum need will have to be imported. The other sheds disclose cooking oil from Algeria, utensils from Romania and a variety of canned goods, cloth, kitchenware, tools, plastic sandals, powdered milk and school materials from Portugal, the USSR, Eastern Europe and the Scandinavian countries. Some are gifts to the PAIGC, donated by friendly countries during the armed struggle, but as these run out, new goods are bought at regular prices on the world market. In one shed several tons of peanuts and palm-nuts are waiting to be exported and in a month's time there should be some cashews as well.

Scattered around the big yard, under mango trees and in a grove of cashews, are piles of oil drums and crates containing engines and spares. Further down lie huge spools of heavy-duty cable. The aging foreman who shows us around is constantly harassed by workers with little slips of paper they want him to sign; some red, some yellow, some green. A long argument accompanies each one and some of the men have to go away without the crucial scribble. The potential for bureaucratic tumors in this place boggles the mind, but so far things seem to be running rather smoothly; at least our friend knows what most things are, where they come from and their destination. A couple of new, sturdy Volvo trucks are being loaded with an assortment of merchandise for the interior. Together with the outfit's nine barges, a fleet of twenty-four of these vehicles are responsible for supplying the entire network of stores. Again, insufficient, but at least enough to keep things going until more material can be acquired. A major part of the transportation problem stems from bad roads and a lack of experienced drivers; the heap of wrecked units down in the far end of the yard tell the sad story.

The People's Store corporation operates under the auspices of the Ministry of Commerce and Crafts and is headed by a twelve-member board with representatives from various other ministries. The workers, too, have one representative. The direct administrative responsibility is with the Director-General, Francisco Coutinho, whose office we find there in the middle of it all. More slips of paper in an impressive spectrum of colors, but an efficient secretary manages to divert most of it before it reaches Coutinho's desk. Here, as well, things appear under control. On two walls are display racks with the full range of items stocked by the *armazens.* We sample Swiss cream cheese which has just arrived; it looks like it has been stored for a long time but tastes fine. The progress made since independence is impressive. First priority remains to extend the network to within easy reach of every village in the country, then to expand the selection of goods. Problems? Yes, in nearly field, particularly transport and long-range planning. Coutinho, however, is optimistic. 'Within three years, maximum, the People's Stores will be capable of supplying the national market with everything the people need and always within the spirit of loyal and healthy competition for which they were created.'

'....loyal and healthy competition...?' Private business has not been nationalized, nor is the Government planning to do so in the near future. The PAIGC are not 'hysterical revolutionaries.' as Frelimo's Samora Machel has commented regarding his government's similar approach to the problems of national reconstruction; they don't intend to tear something down before they have something to put in its place. And it will be quite some time yet before the *armazens do povo* could carry the entire load of national commerce. Meanwhile, the Government appears satisfied to assert some control, to 'discipline economic activity.' Private and State enterprise co-exist within this framework: the People's Stores corporation has a monopoly on the import of all 'primary' necessities' and acts as wholesaler to private merchants who wish to carry such items at a price of cost plus twenty per cent. In this way retail prices can be kept lower than before while the merchants and the People's Stores both gain an 'acceptable' share, said to be twenty per cent over wholesale. The effect: 'Profits are rigorously controlled and speculation gains no ground; the market is disciplined on the basis of people's needs and the capability of the State,' according to Coutinho. Later, the regime will take further steps to ensure that, for instance, desperately short foreign exchange is utilized in line with the country's developmental needs. Says Armando Ramos, 'We hope that our stores will soon be able to import all the things essential to Guine's economic development. Gradually, we plan to take control over the entire foreign trade.'

This will inevitably mean a radical change in import and consumption patterns, especially for the better-off sectors of Bissau's population. During the war an ever-increasing portion of the colony's foreign currency went to import goods that can only be characterized as luxuries, given the country's situation: wines and liquors, private cars, stereo sets - all items to meet the inflated needs of a privileged minority. But such a reorientation will no doubt mean a political struggle. 'In fact, many problems are concentrated here in Bissau,' continues Ramos. 'Money used to flow in as a consequence of the war. Life in Bissau was one of abundance and there was little awareness of the fact that this was taking place at the expense of our brothers who sacrificed themselves for the struggle....The population of Bissau will now be obliged to sacrifice a little too for the reconstruction of our country.' So far, the import of luxury items has not been stopped. It is, however, becoming subject to rapidly rising customs rates and taxes. While three months ago a measure of whiskey cost about the same as a can of ginger ale, produced in Bissau, it is now twice as much. This revenue will be channeled into the expansion of the People's Stores system and the subsidization of internal transport so as to maintain a single level of prices throughout the country, an added incentive to Bissau's many unemployed and idle to move back to their villages.

The merchants, then, how are they taking this? Coutinho ponders the question. 'I think we can say that the big companies like Gouvea and Ultramarina* have retreated without manifesting any clear opposition. As for the small and middle merchants, they are more and more coming to understand their new social role as complimenting our stores and our mutual transactions increase each day.' Armando Ramos, on the other hand, has directed a public 'appeal' to the merchants 'to become conscious of the difficult phase our country is passing through, so as to avoid confrontation wherever possible.... Otherwise we will have to turn to other means, more drastic and vio lent, but still just. Perhaps this is the only way our merchants will comprehend that this is not the moment to amass hugh profits...to the detriment of those who gave so much to help liberate our coun-

* *Casa Gouvea,* a large chain of shops owned by the huge *Compania Uniao Fabril* of Lisbon and *Sociedade Comercial Ultramarina,* another large trading company. Between them, these two giants controlled more than fifty per cent of the private trade in Guine before the war.

try.'

On the surface things are smooth. Shop windows are decorated with photos of Amilcar Cabral and the national colors while this year's May Day parade, the first ever to be held in Bissau, featured the unusual sight of shopkeepers walking alongside their workers, denouncing the exploitation of man by man in a touching display of 'solidarity.' But how far will they go? Some of the large companies may well close shop with their owners and managers returning to Portugal. Others, particularly the less wealthy, will most likely continue, if at all possible: their alternatives are few and most have not much to retire on. In any case, it's doubtful that any of them will try to repeat the sabotage campaign of six months ago. If they do, they will find themselves confronted with both a government determined to use State power to improve the people's conditions of life and the people themselves, increasingly conscious and ready to assume greater control over their own lives.

A New Spirit of Justice

Oppressed peoples do not emerge 'pure' and untouched from the forge of imperialist exploitation. Many problems and conflicts remain. These are largely 'contradictions among the people,' contradictions between the new social order and the heritage of colonialism and negative traditions. In Guinea-Bissau, the resolution of such contradictions is the essential task of the Department of Justice. Its method is political mass mobilization and the work goes far beyond the range of activity that Europeans and North Americans associate with the legal profession.

Vicente Monteiro is a husky, soft-spoken man in his early forties. Like so many other PAIGC militants, he is hardly ever seen without his zig-zag pattern wollen *cofio* cap, in other West African countries a Muslim symbol, but in Guinea-Bissau a way of associating the owner with the memory of Amilcar Cabral who, by so often wearing one, gave it a new meaning. Monteiro may wear his with pride. In mid-1963 he was in the first tiny group of guerrillas who under the command of Osvaldo Vieira and armed with three automatics, arrived here in the bush near Mores village to open the North Front against the numerous and well-equipped Portuguese. 'The first months were dangerous,' he recalls, 'even if we took the *tugas* by surprise. The problem was that we hardly knew what we were doing.' For emphasis he holds up his left hand. It's half gone, leaving only the thumb and the index finger in a crooked position. 'An improvised mine; it went off as I was trying to plant it. . . . After that, we left explosives to the specialists.'

For Monteiro, however, the accident marked the end of active combat. He spent some twelve painful hours before a medic could be found, then a few months of treatment and recuperation in neighboring Senegal. In the years following he worked with the movement's Conakry-based information services and as a political commissar in the South. 'So I was in a good position to help introduce the People's Tribunals when they were started in 1969.' Today he is the *responsavel* for justice in the central region of Oio, densely populated and the scene of heavy military confrontation throughout the war. By 25 April and the ceasefire the liberated areas of Oio had a well organized administrative apparatus, including 27 local - village or section - tribunals. In theory, these are still functioning, but with people now leaving their wartime forest shelters for their old *tabancas* and thousands of refugees returning from the North, some reorganization is necessary. New judges must be elected to replace those who have left and the particular problems resulting from migration and resettlement must be taken care of.

This is plenty to keep Vicente Monteiro busy. When we first meet at Mores, he's about to set out on a tour of six nearby villages to see if all positions are filled and discuss the work of the tribunals with the villagers. He is accompanied by Tijane, a youthful fighter-turned-commissar after he, too, was wounded, losing his left arm to a NATO-supplied howitzer. Together they remind us of the incredible hardship and determination that were so characteristic of this forest war.

A courier has already left; throughout the trip he'll be one village ahead of Monteiro and Tijane, notifying the local Party committees and helping organize mass meetings. As walking is the only way of getting around - there are neither cars nor roads - one village a day is all they will be able to cover.

One week later, just as dusk gives way to the impenetrable blackness of the Oio night, they are back - tired, dirty and hungry after walking eleven miles since completing the day's work at Iracunda *tabanca*. Tomorrow there will be one last meeting here in Mores before Monteiro moves on to another zone. Things have gone well, he confides over our evening meal of curried rice. No significant cases to report; only the administrative business, mass meetings and minor disputes which are easily settled. However, with all the refugees coming back, he expects an increase in the number of conflicts over land, animals, and other property. 'The war really upset the old patterns and we're bound to see some friction before life settles in its new mold. But I'm sure we'll be able to cope as they have done in the other regions.' In this sense, his present task is of a preventive nature; by calling meetings to discuss problems and new Government policies much of the potential friction is brought out and resolved before it can cause much harm.

About two hundred of the villagers have gathered for the Mores meeting; men on one side, women and babies on the other. In front stands a table with a few chairs for Monteiro and the village tribunal members. As they take their seats, talking ceases and latecomers find themselves a space on the ground. Monteiro speaks in Creole, occassionally glancing down at his battered notebook while Tijane translates into Oxinca, the local Mandinga dialect. His first point concerns the replacement of a judge who has left. Since the remaining incumbents are both men, Monteiro suggests the people consider a woman for the vacant seat. Government policy, he underlines, insists that there be at least one female judge on each tribunal. Then the subject of sexual violation, not direct rape which is rare and severely punished, but the fact that 'men often use unmarried women to please themselves without taking responsibility.' This is quite in keeping with traditional custom which offers women little protection unless they 'belong' to another man. Such behavior, informs Monteiro, can have no place in the new Guine.

Next comes the need to completely liquidate theft and fighting among villagers. Moreover, it is now against the law to severely beat or kill other people's animals when they destroy crops or do other harm. Instead, a judge should be called to assess the damage for which the animal's owner will be held responsible. If this law can be respected, a major source of conflict within the *tabancas* will be removed.

Also, as Mores now has its own school, parents should see to it that their children really attend classes and not just leave them to do as they wish. This, to be sure, goes for daughters too; the common attitude that girls have no use for schooling is counter to the spirit of progress that the Party stands for.

Finally, a touchy subject: land tenure and the conflicts between traditional rights and current needs. Here in Oio people grow their rice by clearing plots in the forest nearby, at a different place every year. Each family holds exclusive rights to tracts of forest large enough to shift around as required. Now, however, returning refugees and newcomers are finding it increasingly hard to get land within a reasonable distance from the village. 'Therefore,' says Monteiro, looking intensely at some of the *homen grandes* as he makes his point, 'those with plenty of land must share with those who have none. Nobody must suffer because he cannot find land to cultivate and, besides, we need to increase production.' Gradually, new methods of cultivation and corresponding land reforms will have to be introduced. In the meantime it is important to get the new people settled and instill a spirit which will help make such reforms effective; to make the villagers themselves initiate the process.

The sun is barely one scorching hour away from zenith by the time Monteiro is through. Pearls of sweat appear from underneath his cap. Tijane has been replaced but takes over again to translate the people's response. First to speak is Binta Seidi, in her late sixties and perhaps the oldest woman in the *tabanca* and highly esteemed. She agrees that they need a female judge; men often see things one-sidedly so it should not be left to them alone to judge everything, especially cases involving women. Sajo Bodja, *homen grande* and chairman of the village committee, gets up next. In principle he too agrees that a woman judge would strengthen the tribunal, but the charge of one-sidedness is unfair. As for the other points, 'it's necessary that we follow the lead of the Party. Only because of the PAIGC did we win our freedom and only by staying with it can we continue our progress.

With this, Monteiro makes the village committee responsible for organizing the election of a third judge and closes the meeting, just in time to catch the daily water truck down to the main road. There he hopes to find transport back to his office in Mansoa and with some luck he'll be home by evening.

This meeting quite well demonstrates the role of the People's Tribunals in mobilizing the population. Only part of their activities lie within the range of work most foreigners would consider as 'jurisprudence.' Their most important role is that of political education and discussion, of introducing new ideas and proposed policies which will be put in the law books only after thorough testing at the local level. If this process can be kept alive, it will form a crucial hedge against the dangers of bureaucratic elitism and 'directivism' which have helped stifle the programs of progressive regimes elsewhere. Of course, a precondition for its continuation is the close interaction between the revolutionary vanguard and the masses, within a framework that ensures and encourages the people's free and creative participation. Guinea-Bissau seems well placed to sustain such a process; the popular character of the PAIGC and the gradual evolution of new and social structures in the liberated areas during the armed struggle are factors which work in a positive direction. Now, much depends on the ability of cadres returning to the bush from outside training, often in foreign universities, to merge their professional knowledge and values with the experience, interests and aspirations of the peasants in the countless *tabancas* at the roots of the Guinea-Bissau revolution.

If the tribunals are already strong in the countryside, they are bound to meet with difficulties among that half of Guine's population who lived under Portuguese control until the very day of independence. Even if PAIGC's impact has been great during the ensuing eight months, the political confusion of the newly liberated is still great. Nevertheless, preparations are underway to introduce popular justice in these urban areas. Each tribunal will be composed of five members, one with juridicial training and four elected by the people. The candidates will have to demonstrate their support for the struggle; they must not be public employees and they must enjoy a certain respect in the community. Naturally, this will take time. In the meantime, the Government has to clean up the mess left by the colonial regime. Totally occupied with imposing military 'justice,' the Portuguese neglected virtually all other legal business for the last six or seven years and as a result, nearly five thousand cases - civil and criminal - awaited the PAIGC when they entered the Bissau courthouse last September; mountains of dusty documents in filing cabinets, cardboard boxes or simply in piles on the floor. Where to start? 'First,' says Joao Cruz Pinto, Solicitor General and one of the Party's first lawyers, 'we created a special commission to handle all this unfinished business. Then another problem developed. . . .' Now that a new legal machinery had been set up, a frustrated public started to bombard the court with cases. Therefore a second commission was set up to deal exclusively with the new work. Portuguese laws were immediately abolished and while waiting for a new code of justice, the commissions base their rulings on the broad premises of traditional conventions, the axioms of the Party and the fundamental principles expressed in the Declaration of Human Rights.

In 'Portuguese' Guine, as in so many other countries, 'real' justice was reserved for the rich. Only they could afford lawyers to look after their interests, not infrequently to the detriment of the less affluent, of course, and always to the material advantage of the men of the 'liberal profession' themselves. Will they have any role in the new system? According to Cruz Pinto, an association will be set up to employ all lawyers with salaries according to qualifications. It will be separate from, though controlled by, the Department of Justice, and clients can still request to be represented by the lawyer of their choice. The fees, which together with a Government subsidy are intended to finance this arrangement, will be determined according to the character of the case and the client's resources. Which means that the poor will receive free or cheap legal aid and the rich will pay correspondingly more.

For the time being, however, the system functions without lawyers; plaintiff, defendant, witnesses, the commission and the court clerks have the courtroom to themselves. On the day we visit four cases are expedited; two women who have fought in the marketplace are reconciled, a divorce is settled, a shopkeeper badly behind in his rent is given a deadline to pay. The final case concerns an improper transaction. An old Portuguese merchant has bought a shoestore from a compatriot who wanted to leave Guine in a hurry. He has paid-up the $11,000 total, but cannot open for business since the seller's rushed departure prevented the legal documents from getting properly processed. With all this capital tied up for six months now, he finds himself in financial trouble - or so he says. The seller has written from Lisbon that he has no intention of coming back to sign anything for 'those PAIGC communists.' But our friend doesn't feel this way. Oh, no; he just wants to open his store. Thirty years in

Guine already and he'd like to stay for the rest of his life. After ten minutes of deliberation, Cruz Pinto, as Head of the commission, calls the merchant to attention and the decision is read out: the shop is now officially his. Just like that, no further judicial rigmarole - and much better treatment than he could ever have expected from the system of which he was so much a part. Wonder what he thinks, this colonial veteran, of these once-so-feared 'terrorists' as he humbly backs out of the courtroom, bowing and scraping all the way?

People's Courts to Serve the People's Interests

In this interview Fidelis Almada, Secretary of Justice, explains how popular traditions combine with the needs of the revolution to provide a legal basis for the new people's power. Negative customs are fought and new ideals are put into practice, all within the context of the continuing ideological struggle that is rapidly helping to transform Guinea-Bissau.

Fidelis Cabral Almada worked clandestinely for the liberation movement as a student in Lisbon. In 1961 he left for Brazil where he passed the bar and worked as a lawyer while representing the PAIGC. Arrested during the military coup in 1964 he was released due to a vigorous international campaign and joined his comrades-in-arms in Guinea-Bissau later that year. After returning from military training in China, Almada was responsible for education on the Northern Front until 1969 when he was given the task of organizing the Party's new Department of Justice.

Comrade Almada, can you outline the origins of the system of justice that is now taking shape in Guinea-Bissau?

In 1966, after three years of war, we wrote our first laws to be used in PAIGC's military tribunals. These tribunals were intended mainly for disciplining our militants and were convened only for the duration of the specific cases. Their main objective was to prevent contradictions from arising between the armed forces and the population as a result of occasional friction and quarrels in the liberated areas.

With larger liberated zones and more people came more quarrels, not so much between the people and the fighters as among the people themselves. Since we had no written law, we settled the most serious disputes in our tribunal of war, our only organ of justice at the time.

Late in 1968 Amilcar Cabral and I began to prepare the establishment of a People's Tribunal and I was assigned the task of organizing it. The military court was necessary while we were fighting, but with the development of the struggle and the increase in the liberated population, it became imperative to organize a more comprehensive system of justice. For instance, fighters and many civilians carried arms. Since many were not used to handling weapons, accidents occurred and we had to have a way to deal with this.

But what kind of tribunal were we to have? Cabral stressed that we should introduce a different kind of justice than our people had experienced under Portuguese occupation when there were laws for Portuguese citizens and a completely different set of laws for the 'indigenous' ninety per cent of the population. These 'indigenous laws' meant nothing, though, since the colonial administrators were free to do as they wished. They tortured and executed people on the verandas of their homes.

The PAIGC needed to prove to the people who had been living under Portuguese law that things were now different. While we had been fighting for a long time, we had no written law, no authority to draft laws and no cadres to administer justice. Therefore, our solution was to be based on our people's traditional customs; therein lies the solution for the quarrels and most other problems of the struggle. The Portuguese had discarded our customs as those of 'wild' people, but we found a way of giving new life to our traditions. Though they are illiterate, the villagers are more familiar with traditional law than I am and so they could elect judges from among themselves.

From the very outset, our Party's goal has been to put power in the hands of our people. To let the population administer justice is very significant because then they begin to realize that the colonialists no longer rule over them. On the contrary, they themselves make justice. In 1969 we organized the first People's Tribunals in the countryside.

When basing the tribunals on traditional law, however, there are problems. For instance, the laws of the different tribes, such as the Balanta and Mandinga, vary a great deal and in places where the tribal composition of the population is mixed, this must have caused confusion.

We solved this problem by imposing the customs of the largest group in each region. For example, in a Balanta-dominated area, all cases are decided on the basis of Balanta tradition whether they are cases between Balanta and, say, Fula or even disputes involving two Fula.

Of course, this means changes. In Balanta custom, for instance, it is more or less a traditional sport to steal cattle. But the Balanta rarely steal alone; groups of young people go rustling together. But if one is caught, he will reveal everything and each member of the group will have to pay one cow each, even if there are as many as ten thieves. Among the Fula, on the other hand, only one cow will have to be returned. So, in a Fula region even the Balanta live by Fula law and vice versa. Everyone has now come to accept this.

There are also some traditions which are reactionary and which violate the principles of our Party. In these cases our principles prevailed. This had to be carefully explained to the population by political commissars and the teachers in the local schools, cadres chosen from the ranks of our militants and who knew what PAIGC stands for. If a people's judge wished to decide a case in violation of our principles, these cadres intervened by explaining the contradiction. Deliberations then continued until an acceptable judgement was passed.

One such negative tradition was in relation to the question of marriage and the position of women. Can you elaborate on that?

In traditional Guinea-Bissau marriage was not a decision for the young people, whose opinion was never asked, but for the parents. Women were valued primarily for their reproductive capacity and their labor power; marriage was a business transaction and young girls were often given to old men who could pay a good dowry rather than to young ones who had had little time to accumulate wealth. Little girls would be married off and after puberty they would go and live with their husbands. The woman had no right to dissent.

Our Party has fought for liberation so as to free everybody, men and women. One consequence of this is that people can no longer be compelled to marry against their will. During the war, in the liberated zones, many betrothed young women raised this question when they became conscious of their new freedom. Even when the parents had arranged a marriage, our laws gave the daughter the right to go to the people's court which would then confirm her freedom. While before she could be brought to her arranged husband by force, now she has the right to choose. In cases where the parents have already received the dowry, the 'buyer' must be compensated by the new husband the girl chooses to marry. However, all this has caused so many complications that the custom of dowry is now starting to disappear.

If we had merely passed a law, there would have been a lot of opposition to these ideas. Instead, our cadres spent a great deal of time discussing the new ideas with the people. Nothing was imposed; we simply let the logic of liberation prevail. Sometimes, when the men protested, we asked them, 'Do you want to be free while women remain in slavery?' In the village meetings nobody dared oppose this principle and so when a practical case came up, it was difficult to resist. Not everybody accepted this willingly, of course, but they do not dare to oppose the practical solution when the political principle is already accepted.

It is the prestige and authority of the PAIGC which have enabled us to make progress in this way. When differences and opposition emerge, they cannot be eliminated by law because the power of tradition is very, very strong. Our cadres have had to struggle with the people, explain and discuss time after time and in this way use the work of the people's courts to advance their political consciousness.

Another important such struggle has been over the question of divorce. With some of the ethnic groups, the man was permitted to repudiate his wife while she could do nothing; it was a male privilege. And the men, of course, had no interest in divorce since they wanted wives to work for them in the fields. So we said that this was not just; if a man can repudiate a woman, why can't a woman refuse to live with a man who abuses her or can no longer fulfill his conjugal obligations? We had many cases like this and after much discussion and struggle, divorce had to be permitted.

Polygamy, too, is in direct opposition to the aims and the principles of the PAIGC. But we understand that this custom has an economic basis, and as long as women do not have economic freedom, we cannot directly outlaw polygamy. First we have to create the conditions for women to become equal in law, in pay and in all other ways. We have to give them education to acquire economic independence.

Still, from the start of the liberation struggle we wanted to discourage polygamy. We therefore prohibited male Party cadres from having more than one wife. We expected our cadres to understand this and set an example. For the rest of the population, on the other hand, we still permit those men who have several wives to go on living with these women. This stand is necessary to maintain the unity between the population and the Party. But since women now have the right to divorce, if a man loses one wife this way, he has no right to marry another to replace her.

What is the basis for your system of punishment?

First, capital punishment was dictated by the conditions of war. The Portuguese sent many spies into our liberated zones to report where our people were hiding and guide the bombers to their targets. To protect the population, we had no choice but to execute such spies. Similarly, if we intend to build a new society, we have to prevent murder. In the war, we killed for the sake of liberation, but we could not allow people in the liberated regions to plot murder against others. It is exactly to stop such practices that we are making revolution.

We still have capital punishment and we are not ashamed to say so because we believe that our people's goals are more important than the life of a murderer or spy. This applies only when the crime is proven to be premeditated. With accidental killings, the penalty is from three months to one year in confinement. We have been very careful to be fair; every judgement in the liberated zones was made in public and proof was submitted until the people were convinced of the guilt of the accused.

During the war we did not have prisons, but we were still able to sentence offenders to perform productive labor. In the south-eastern part of our country which was safe from enemy ground incursions, we set up recuperation camps - here the convicts grew rice, built houses for our fighters and transported supplies for our forces. The prisoners had a political organization where they elected their own leaders. These recuperation camps were schools of political education. The prisoners engaged in criticism and self-criticism and many became Party militants while in the camps. They examined the causes of their crimes and they could also criticize any aspect of the operation of the camp and our cadres who ran it. The prisoners were well treated and we had very few cases of escape. They were given food, clothes, shoes, soap - everything necessary to live in the same conditions as our guerrillas.

You said earlier that the political consciousness which developed in the liberated areas was important in advancing the work of the people's tribunals. But here in Bissau you find yourself in a different situation.

Yes, a very different situation. This is why we have not yet organized local tribunals here in Bissau. First we have to organize the people and create political committees in the various communities. As political activity develops, we will be able to find people to serve as judges in the urban centers. This is how we worked in the liberated areas and it is the best way to proceed because the initial level of political consciousness is often very low. Here in Bissau, some people still have a fascist mentality and an inclination toward corruption. Our solution is to begin organizing them.

You have faced a range of problems since you arrived in this city.

Drug abuse for instance, was common. How have you approached this kind of problem?

The social problems here were great. Many young people were corrupted with drugs and alcohol. There were nightclubs, wild drinking, and rampant prostitution. When the Portuguese left, many people who had worked in the war economy became unemployed because we were unable to absorb them all. Crime was so frequent that it was dangerous to walk in the streets. Many of the 17,000 young people who have served in the colonial army kept their weapons and literally terrorized the city population night and day.

We had to be tough in the face of this situation. Those criminals who import and sell drugs may now be executed; our national assembly has passed a law to that effect. Those who only use drugs are victims and are sent to a recuperation center. We have transformed the former Portuguese prison here in Bissau into such a center, based on the model of those in the liberated zones.

We have clamped down on theft as well. Convicted thieves are sent to distant rural areas to work in the fields under the responsibility of the local village committees. A few weeks after our military forces had taken control over Bissau, the streets were safe once more.

Today, all prisoners receive political education in accordance with the principles of our recuperation camps. We are planning to create a special cooperative where we can send convicted criminals for agricultural training. We don't intend to put people in jails, but send them to work in production. Even those who must be kept here in Bissau, will be trained in a useful profession.

You face a great shortage of cadres here in the Department of Justice. Most of the people in this building are civil servants trained by the colonial administration. Doesn't this make it difficult to develop your new system of justice?

Yes, among the one hundred employees here only Joao Cruz Pinto and I are Party militants, so both of us have to work as political commissars. We have begun to organize the Department with special meetings every two weeks to analyze our tasks. Everybody attends these meetings and we make use of criticism and self-criticism to improve our punctuality, conscientiousness and general work discipline. This, of course, is new to everyone on the staff but things have started to change. For instance, the section heads did not respect the people who cleaned the toilets. They treated them like dogs. Today we encourage our janitors to criticize anyone; they can criticize me, too, when I make a mistake or if they disagree with me.

Once a month we have a general meeting with everybody working in the field of justice in the entire Bissau region. Our discussion centers around the principles of the Party and how they apply to our work. We have also organized volunteer work on Sundays. I suggested to the heads of the different sections that they should be the first to respond to this call and, indeed, they came and performed physical labor. This would have been inconceivable under colonialism.

I try to lead by setting an example. I try to be the first to arrive in the morning and at six o'clock, when our work day ends, I take care not to rush away. I tell my co-workers that we need to take on many tasks in order to begin to develop our country. In this way I am helping to change their mentality.

What kind of criticisms have been raised at your Department meetings?

The main criticism has been directed at the bad attitude of the office chiefs toward those whom they regarded as their servants. When I first came here, there were daily quarrels between the functionaries because of this. Then there has been the problem of competition; everyone wanted to make more money but they were not concerned with the advancement of our system of justice. We have also taken up the problem of 'employee mentality': indifference and lack of creativity in our work. Before, everyone tried to look busy when the chief walked in, but as soon as he turned his back, they would sit back and chat. Now, as a consequence of higher political consciousness, we have started to work more productively.

You are working on a new code of justice. Guinea-Bissau, at this stage, is still plotting its new course through a sea of great economic and social problems and sharp class contradiction. How does this affect your planning for the future?

From the beginning of the struggle our aim has been to put political power in the hands of our people, represented by the PAIGC. Our new code of justice will be one way of making this possible. There is no such thing as universal justice; that notion is utopian. The system of justice which was organized under colonial fascist domination was designed to protect the interests of the colonial bourgeoisie. Now we are organizing our justice to serve the working classes.

True, there are still sharp class contradictions in Guinea-Bissau. In the countryside, some landowners and chiefs have a typical capitalist mentality, but this is not a serious contradiction at this time. In the towns, however, we have major problems with the petty bourgeoisie - merchants, functionaries, clerical workers - who for a long time have lived and worked under colonialism. As Amilcar Cabral wrote, Guinea-Bissau has no classical bourgeoisie with economic power and resultant class consciousness. And with no industry, we have no developed working class. But we do have tendencies, an embryonic working class and an embryonic bourgeoisie with strong capitalist aspirations and values. We believe we can resolve class contradictions of this nature with protracted and intensive political work. Every day we have confrontations, but we are confident that we will win this second struggle: the struggle for economic progress with its political-ideological battles in which we are now engaged.

Justice plays a very important part in this ideological struggle. Our justice has the aim of helping to transform our society. Therefore our justice, a popular justice, must be based on a clear understanding of our people and our political aims. We prefer preventive justice to repressive justice; to prevent crime we have to have social justice. This is why the administration of justice is in every way political work and forms but one aspect of the work of our Party.

The Great Knowledge Offensive

'...The system itself has changed but our objectives remain the same. We are expanding education in every field in order to accelerate the creation of the 'new human being' that Amilcar Cabral so often talked about.'

Mario Cabral, Secretary of Education and Culture

We get our first impression of the new Guinea-Bissau already in Lisbon while we're awaiting our flight to Bissau. On 11 March (1975), the same day that General Spinola and his supporters in the military unsuccessfully try to seize power, our small downtown boarding house suddenly fills up with young PAIGC militants who have come to Portugal for teacher's training. They are excited over the events of the day - if the coup had succeeded, they wouldn't have stayed long - and by the fact of having arrived in a strange country that is to be home for the next three years.

This is the first group of Guinean students to arrive under a recent agreement between the new Portuguese and PAIGC governments; young men and women of the 'Amilcar Cabral generation,' the first age group to have truly grown up with the liberation movement and the armed struggle. Their education so far has been acquired under primitive conditions, in bush schools supplemented by brief courses at the 'pilot schools' outside. But their schooling has been an integral part of the struggle; they have worked the land, carried supplies and even taught those with less training than themselves. Some have been fighters, others medics or political workers, because this was - and still is - the essence of PAIGC's educational philosophy: integrate book learning with the lives and culture of the people; mold cadres to serve the interests of the masses. It was not a matter of abstract principle, it was the only basis on which the population could be mobilized and the concrete tasks of liberation accomplished, the only way to push the struggle forward.

PAIGC's educational achievements during the war became well known. With an almost totally illiterate peasant population, the question of education was crucial right from the start and thus, at the First Party Congress in early 1964, the decision was made to establish schools in the still small but rapidly expanding liberated areas. Almost anyone with book knowledge passed as a teacher. 'It was quite something,' recalls Inacio Semedo who, with his high school background from Portugal, was in a better position than most. 'When Cabral returned from the Congress and told us we were to teach, we didn't know what to think. Now, looking back, it's clear to me that those eight months I spent in the bush of Cubucare turned my whole life around.' For people like Inacio, of *assimilado* or petty bourgeois background, such experiences were the first steps in the long and difficult process of 'class suicide.' For the villagers, locked into their narrow, traditional universe, the establishment of schools, even if strictly rudimentary, was a decisive step in conquering the barriers of mental oppression.

By mid-1964 there might have been a few hundred students in these bush schools. Ten years later their number had swelled to 15,000, two-thirds of whom were in first or second grade. For those who were selected to continue beyond the four years of primary education, there were the two Party pilot schools in the Republic of Guinea and Senegal with a joint capacity of about five hundred students toward the end of the war. After that came university or specialized training in Cuba, Yugoslavia, the Soviet Union, GDR or other friendly countries. Already during the first precarious years of the war, at a time when anyone with schooling was desperately needed inside, PAIGC began to send students overseas in what might have seemed like a fit of optimism. The investment, however, started paying off toward the end of the sixties as the now skilled cadre gradually returned to take on the mounting tasks of armed struggle and national reconstruction. But only after they had spent some time at the Political-Military Training Center where they found themselves in class with combatants receiving basic literacy training and political education. 'At first some of us may have found this degrading,' concedes Mario Cabral, today Secretary of Education and Culture but in 1971 fresh with a doctorate from Lisbon where he had organized clandestine activities. 'There you were, side by side with someone who couldn't read, perhaps not even speak Creole. But let me tell you, this was *real* training; absolutely necessary to wash out our elitism and learn to work effectively among the people.'

Thus the PAIGC's educational system cannot be evaluated by its scholastic standards alone. In fact, more important than purely academic standing was the students' ability to play a positive political role and contribute concretely to the armed struggle and (the process of) national reconstruction. In this respect, independence has made little difference. Says Mario Cabral, 'The system itself may have changed, but our objectives remain the same. We are expanding education in every field to accelerate the creation of 'the new human being' that Amilcar Cabral used to talk so much about.'

'This is an aspect foreign to those of us who drifted through European and North American schools only to 'get ahead' in life - ahead of the others, that is. The contrast between what the two of us knew from home as 'school' and what we experienced in Guine - in classrooms, at cultural events, talking to students and teachers during time off or joining in games of barefoot soccer - is of such a magnitude that it will take time to sink in. But already, the idea of sending our children to the run-of-the-mill American school is less than appealing. Frankly, it never dawned on us what a powerful tool education really can be until we witnessed, at close range, this process of the 'new human being' in the making.

Take the Areolino Cruz School at Cufar. Until one month before our visit this boarding school was located in the bush of Tombali region where it had been moving around since first established in 1966. Then, with the departure of the Portuguese, it became possible to settle down. Cufar airstrip, big enough for 707's, used to be the southern base of the colonialist air force. From here their Fiat jets could be anywhere in the South within a few minutes. Now the runway lies naked and unswept, barbed wire and half-collapsed machine-gun nests all around. Our young driver takes the opportunity to test the jeep; nowhere else in this country can you do seventy and yet be sure to arrive safely

We find the school in the installations at the far end. The state of the place says something about what morale and conditions must have been like among the Portuguese forces: wrecked trucks and machinery all over, mountains of rusty cans, ammunition boxes and spent cartridges, heaps of moldy, spoilt supplies in the abandoned storage sheds. Evidently the *tugas* didn't give a damn when they finally packed it in. Yet, with hard work and much imagination the teachers and students together have made the camp livable. Four huts have been turned into classrooms with long tables, a teacher's desk and a blackboard in each. A tiny chapel has had its Catholic paraphernalia removed and now serves as library. The boys live four to a room in the smaller huts while the girls are lodged three in each room of what must have been the officers' quarters. Austerity and order; every room is tidy, the bunks neatly made and the few personal belongings in the closets or boxes under the beds.

Like all of PAIGC's boarding schools, the Cufar school is run by Friendship Institute, an institution created for this purpose, and many of the students are orphans or children of Party militants. The school looks after everybody's needs, even if some receive a few small things from home once in a while. Care is taken that no great differences arise; that, for instance, nobody has two pairs of good shoes and others only the usual plastic sandals donated by a foreign government. No money is allowed. 'As it is,' explains Dinis Cabelol, the 24-year old director, 'the students have no need for cash and it would create just the kind of inequalities we are trying to avoid.'

There are close to two hundred students at Cufar, forty of whom are girls. All activities are organized by student committees with the teachers serving as advisors. There is plenty to do other than the regular school work. Some groups take turns in the kitchen and dining hall where, for the time being, there are neither tables nor chairs, as they were needed to furnish the classrooms. Others are responsible for keeping the living quarters clean and still others for the arduous task of removing the trash left by the Portuguese. A few boys are helping a carpenter repair the huts.

Still, Dinis is apologetic for not having achieved more. 'Only next year will we be ready to grow our own food. Self-sufficiency is a high priority with us; we consume three tons of riçe a month and now all of it has to be imported.' The food storage room is filled with bags of beans and powdered milk as well as huge cans of cooking oil. To supplement these staples the school employs a hunter and a fisherman. Later we meet the tailor who, with the help of three of the senior students, works hard at turning bales of blue cloth into school uniforms. The only one we miss is the school nurse who has accompanied Dinis' wife to the Catio hospital to deliver the couple's first-born.

Life at the other boarding schools we visit is essentially the same as at Cufar. At Mores, in the North, the students spend four hours every day helping a crew of workers construct the new school buildings. For the time being they are lodged in tents and temporary shelters which will offer but little protection once the rainy season gets underway.

The new Mores school is located near a grove of cashew trees where lie buried dozens of Portuguese soldiers, victims of their own commander's success when he, in 1964, had them penetrate this PAIGC stronghold with no possibilities for retreat. At night the students organize their *culturas,* sessions of dance, songs and theater, on top of the mass grave. The scene takes on a strong element of symbolism: only over the bodies of dead Portuguese could spring this new generation of politically conscious and active Guineans; only by shattering old, oppressive structures could this people finally start tapping the great source of human potential in their midst. Of course, nothing unique for Guinea-Bissau, this; the same potential lies latent in every people. But it is only when we see what *can* be done that we become fully aware of what a crime against humanity capitalist oppression really is, whether in its colonial or some other cloak.

Aged seven to seventeen, in the classrooms or at the construction site, dancing or studying in silence at night under the Mores 'street' lights with a million insects fluttering above; they are the cadres of tomorrow. To ensure their development they live under the same conditions and are on duty 24 hours a day, 7 days a week. The cadres of today, the teachers, are in some cases hardly older than their pupils. At Cufar there are six, at Bedanda four, and at Mores seven. About half are high school students recruited by the Government after Independence, the others are Party militants. Their salary is the same, $150 a month. The Directors are all people who have proven their reliability in the struggle. Here is Nino Djata, at twenty responsible for the entire Mores school: 'In 1964 some friends told me about the war and the Party. Soon after we walked for three days to the Sara region to join. I didn't tell my parents since they would have opposed it.' They probably would; in 1964 Nino was nine years old! At Sara he was put in school where he was taught by, among others, our interpreter, Sana na N'Hada, thirteen at the time but hardly any bigger than little Nino. We all laugh as they refresh old memories: stalky legs, swollen bellies, aspiring guerrillas but not even strong enough to hold a rifle straight. In 1968, after four years of schooling, Nino spent three months at the Conakry pilot school before starting as teacher at the Sara hospital. Later he returned to Conakry to complete fifth grade and was transferred to Mores in 1972. He hopes to continue his own education some day, but for the time being he can think of nothing but getting this school properly organized. Only last week forty students from the Candjambari school arrived as part of a plan to centralize the system.

Like Dinis at Cufar, Nino alone is responsible for the political education lessons. The guidelines are set down by the Government, but since there are no books, a lot is left to the initiative of the individual cadre. 'I try to share my experiences with the students,' says Nino. He listens to the radio and reads whatever papers and magazines that find their way to Mores, taking notes. 'Today I told the youngest ones about some of the problems of our State. They tend to think that with Independence anything is possible.' With the older students he concentrates on discussing the policies of the Party and Government.

Certainly, political education is by no means limited to these lessons; to us, every single aspect of school life seemed intensely political. And considering the material limitations, primarily the great lack of supplies, the results are amazing. The students' attitude, for instance; not only in terms of work discipline and commitment to their people, but also in their inquisitive spirit toward the universe beyond - Europe, America, Viet Nam; what could we tell them about this? Arriving at one school, late for lunch, we make a hurried tour of the classrooms for a quick look. Not good enough. Out in the yard, our eyes already focussed on the colossal rice pot which serves the whole school pupulation, we are intercepted; will we please come back and explain who we are and what brings us to Guinea-Bissau?

Our feeling of inadequacy soon dissipates as we strain to convey the distant reality of North American life to the packed classroom. What is LSM, why do we support liberation movements, what are the problems and contradictions of Americans and Canadians? When we draw a rough map to illustrate, they immediately copy it in their exercise books - the school has no maps. The crunch comes in answering questions about 'the youth organization' and the Party schools in our country. In the end we receive a request: can we put them in touch with a school that has more supplies and materials than it needs? We promise to try, with pleasure when we think how good it would do a lot of American school children to establish contact with students like these.

Impressive as they are, the PAIGC boarding schools are not representative of the embryonic national education system. The large majority of Guinea-Bissau's students are to be found in the village schools where problems typical to Third World countries are more visible: the desperate teacher shortage, continued dependence on colonial texts and, not least, the long battle to make school a part of the population's everyday life. The strength and prestige of PAIGC no doubt gives Guinea-Bissau an advantage in the struggle to get children to school, but even at that, it can only be accomplished gradually, step by step as the people's consciousness reaches higher levels. Primary education may be made mandatory, very well, but if the villagers don't understand why, coercion alone can't make the law effective. So the subject is brought up at practically every public meeting we attend and by every political commissar we know.

Still we see groups of children around the villages while the schools remain half empty. For someone who has grown up with school as an unquestionable fact of life, dismay comes easily in such a situation. The PAIGC cadres, however, can never allow themselves such a reaction; impatience and resignation are equally dangerous attitudes. 'You must remember that until very recently our people had every reason to stay away. The schools, where they existed, were mainly tools to impose Portuguese 'civilization.' To mobilize the people, we must dissociate ourselves from this tradition.' A village teacher explains to us the ABC of mass work as patiently as he would explain to the Fula family heads the need for their grandchildren to study rather than to help in the fields. The method is proven by its achievements: after six months the local primary school and adult literacy classes are both showing a marked increase in attendance.

Of ninety per cent peasant background but greatly transformed in the course of the armed struggle, trading the hoe for the gun, the *tabanca* for a life constantly on the move, the thousands of FARP militants are among those whose lives are most immediately affected by independence. As we see them on guard duty, going by in truck loads or simply taking an off-duty stroll, the obvious question becomes: What now? The transition from mobile bush warfare to a stationary barrack existence has not been altogether easy; though they never openly admit it, many are bored by the long hours of guarding public buildings or boot training in the camps. Will they stay in the forces? Most simply shrug; who knows? If they're needed, yes; if not, well....

FARP's new role is still on the drawing board. Clearly, its military task will be vastly different from that of the past and, in addition, it is envisaged playing a prominent part in national reconstruction, providing skill and manpower for agricultural work, road construction and in other tasks. For this a large portion of the present force will be needed. But those who are not? Some have been fighting for more than ten years and cannot be easily re-integrated into village life; a massive demobilization would surely create a lot of rootless men.

One of the FARP's first objectives, therefore, is to upgrade the skills of its troops, both those who will stay and those who will later return to civilian life. 'We are starting with the illiterates,' says Boubakar Barry, one of the army's literacy teachers. 'You know, even though we tried to give everyone some schooling during the war, conditions were difficult and so many of the comrades still have to start from scratch.' The immediate obstacle is, again, the lack of instructors. Many of those with schooling were released to work in the civilian administration and thus FARP has had to call in outside help. In Bissau, secondary school teachers have volunteered to run three-month intensive courses for those militants with some scholastic background so that the latter can serve as instructors to the other combatants. In fact, the first such group of 150 was recently dispersed to the garrisons throughout the country. Later, in a few years, other kinds of training will be introduced: carpentry, mechanics, basic agronomy; skills in line with Guinea-Bissau's developmental priorities and which will make the FARP militants a significant force whether they stay in the military or return to civilian life.

Back in Bissau the struggle takes on other dimensions. Several hundred youth are gathered outside the only high school, Liceu Kwame N'Krumah, for a rally organized by JAAC, the national youth organization. The light morning haze has cleared and the merciless sun goes to work as the speakers take turns at the rostrum. The crowd grows restless; some seek protection under the slender poplars circling the yard. Then it is Carmen Pereira's turn to speak; aggressive and eloquently forceful as always, she jolts the lethargic crowd back to life: 'We too have taken a lot of sun. During twelve years of struggle we suffered the sun so that now we can appreciate the shade of our national flag.' The rally is back on track.

The *liceu* group is also a product of colonial development - but on the opposite end from the villagers of the interior. Predominantly for young Portuguese or the sons of the African petty bourgeoisie, the institution was the main recruiting ground for the colonial administration and a kingpin in Spinola's 'better Guine' scheme, designed to create a native 'cushion' between the African masses and the colonialists proper. In a spirit of supreme elitism, a few African students were groomed to serve the system that would oppose them to the interests of their own people.

Radical change does not come easy to an institution like this. While hardly anyone will openly stand by the fallen regime, deflection seems to be the response of many; live it up as always and keep clear of the critical issues; wriggle your way through.

We also find, of course, the omnipresent 'chameleons,' *liceu* version, the kind who have read some Marx and Lenin since the Lisbon coup and now revel in 'working-class' rhetoric. But Carmen will not be fooled: 'The main contradiction here is between those who sacrificed everything, including their own lives, in the liberation struggle and the opportunists who are interested in nothing but their own big bellies.' The 'blood-suckers,' 'Cafe Imperium coffee flies,' 'snobs' and their cohorts have already been properly denounced by previous speakers. The crowd responds with enthusiasm: 'Down with snobism! Down with the chameleons! Down with the bourgeois opportunists!' We recognize some of the 'coffee flies' nearby as they indignantly wave their fists with the others; down with them, down!

If the approach here is more direct, it is not because the target is less important. 'With the Youth Lies the Future of Our Nation,' proclaims a JAAC banner up front. Indeed, and this includes the *liceu* youth. 'The young are the great majority within our Party,' Mario Cabral points out later, 'and they have been the radicalizing force.' But as certain elements have been 'corrupted by colonialism,' a 'purification' is necessary. 'For the future, we are less interested in the quantity than the quality of our doctors, engineers and lawyers. Above all, we must assure ourselves that they will work for our people and not only for individual gain.'

From this perspective the Party and Government has launched an educational and ideological offensive. The high school now runs in three shifts, morning, afternoon and evening, largely staffed by Portuguese teachers recently arrived under the terms of the assistance agreement. One group, integrated with PAIGC militants, is at work to elaborate new curricula for the entire educational system. The recent opening of long-sealed Lisbon archives will finally make it possible to penetrate colonialist mythology and write an accurate history of both Guine and the other former Portuguese colonies. Political education aims primarily at introducing the students to the history and politics of the liberation movement and is conducted exclusively by Party cadres. JAAC's most important role so far has been to organize collective work Sundays when students join non-students in clearing brush or demolishing abandoned strategic villages. This way Mario Cabral hopes to create an environment that will provide the kind of intellectuals Guinea-Bissau so badly needs. 'I'm confident that the great majority of these students will come our way. But not automatically.' Thus the rallies, slogans, the intense struggle.

The great educational offensive is only getting underway. There are many plans, but none so rigid they cannot be changed. As is repeatedly emphasized, it is still very much a learning process in which mistakes are certain to be made. The crucial task is therefore to establish a framework which will enhance a process of testing and rectification, always in close interaction with those whose interests the system is to serve. Quality before quantity; yet they have to increase the numbers. Projections are being made for a university in the town of Bolama and Mario Cabral hopes to see another two secondary schools in the interior next year. Aren't they getting carried away? 'Why?' He smiles at the visitors' cautious scepticism. 'During the armed struggle almost every new step we took was based on a great deal of optimism. But through determination and struggle we achieved what at first seemed far out of reach. To continue, to realize our aims, we must preserve this determination, this spirit of struggle.'

Glossary

assimilado	black or mixed-race person recognized as 'civilized' by the colonial authorities.
bairro	urban neighborhood or part of town.
chefe do posto	the lowest ranking colonial administrator in the countryside.
cipaio	African assistant to the Portuguese colonial administrators.
comandos africanos	units of specially trained African soldiers who served with the colonialist forces.
FARP	People's Armed Revolutionary Forces.
FLING	Front for the Liberation and National Independence of Guine.
JAAC	*Juventude Africana Amilcar Cabral;* the PAIGC youth organization.
kana	liquor distilled from rice.
moranca	group of huts housing one family unit within Balanta villages.
PIDE	the International Police for the Defense of the State; the now-disbanded Portuguese security police.
pirogue	dug-out canoe.
UNTG	the National Union of Guinean Workers; the Guinea-Bissau trade union organization.

Chronology of Events in Guinea Bissau's Liberation Struggle

1959	Some fifty striking dockworkers are killed and hundreds wounded by Portuguese forces at Pidjiguiti on 3 August. At the first conference of PAIGC cadres held secretly the following month it was resolved to prepare for struggle by all possible means, develop unity through and around the Party, prepare cadres for leadership and, above all, mobilize and organize the peasant masses. August 3rd has since been made Day of International Solidarity with the People of Guinea-Bissau and Cape Verde Islands.
1961	The Conference of Nationalist Organizations in the Portuguese Colonies (CONCP) is founded in Casablanca on 18 April. Member organizations include PAIGC, MPLA, and FRELIMO. An important internationalist structure uniting the three liberation movements.
1963	PAIGC launches its first attacks deep inside Guinea-Bissau on 1 January. The armed struggle spreads rapidly and by the end of June this year PAIGC extends its military activities into the northern region of the country.
1964	On 13 February the First Conference of PAIGC to be held in the liberated areas of Guinea-Bissau opens. The Conference resolved to create the People's Revolutionary Armed Forces (FARP), integrating the operations of the existing Regular Army and Popular Militia. This same month the battle of Como starts when Portuguese forces attempt to expel PAIGC from this island which was liberated in February 1963. After 75 days of fierce fighting the Portuguese colonialist forces withdraw leaving behind more than 600 dead and large amounts of equipment. One of the most crushing defeats inflicted upon colonial troops anywhere in Africa.

1970 In a desperate attempt to overcome serious setbacks within Guinea-Bissau, a Portuguese mercenary force of 300 invades the Republic of Guinea bordering Guinea-Bissau. The objective is to overthrow the progressive government of President Sekou Toure which supports the PAIGC and intimidate African states bordering Angola and Mozambique which support the Liberation Movements. The invasion is decisively repulsed.

1971 PAIGC forces launch their first direct attack on Bissau, capital city of Guinea-Bissau on 9 June. On 26 June, Bafata, second largest town in the country, is also attacked, demonstrating the rapid deterioration of Portuguese control in the territory.

1972 A Special Mission of the UN Committee on Decolonization visits the liberated areas of southern Guinea-Bissau April 2 - 8. Following its visit the Committee recognized PAIGC as 'the only authentic representative of the people of the Territory,' a recognition which was later accepted by the UN General Assembly.

1972 For the first time in the history of the country general elections are carried out in the liberated regions of Guinea-Bissau between the end of August and 14 October, completing a major step in the establishment of the People's National Assembly. At the same time extensive rioting among the people of Cape Verde forces the colonial regime to declare a 'State of Emergency' throughout the archipelago.

1973 On 20 January Amilcar Cabral, founder and Secretary General of PAIGC is treacherously assassinated by agents of Portuguese colonialism.

1973 A heavy PAIGC military offensive results in the capture of the key Portuguese fort of Guiledje on 25 May. At the same time the colonialist command is forced to ground its air force because of the large number of planes hit by PAIGC anti-aircraft fire during the preceding months.

1973 The Second National Congress of PAIGC meets in liberated Guinea-Bissau July 18 - 22. Comrade Aristides Pereira is unanimously elected Secretary-General.

1973 The People's National Assembly convenes in the Boe region, September 23 - 24, and proclaims the Republic of Guinea-Bissau.

1974 Progressive elements of the Portuguese armed forces topple the fascist Lisbon regime on 25 April. Contacts between the new Portuguese government and PAIGC result in an immediate cease-fire as negotiations for the complete withdrawal of colonial presence get under way.

1974 On 26 August Portuguese and PAIGC delegations sign a joint statement declaring that Portugal will formally recognize the independence of the Republic of Guinea-Bissau on 10 September. With the cease-fire still in effect, the colonial administration is rapidly dismantled. By the end of October, Guinea-Bissau is under the full control of its own people, led by PAIGC.

Resources

Chaliand, Gerard. *Armed Struggle in Africa.* New York: Monthly Review Press, 1969.

CIDAC, *Guine-Bissau: 3 annos de independencia.* Lisbon, CIDAC, 1976.

Davidson, Basil, *The Liberation of Guine.* Harmondsworth: Penguin African Library, 1969.

Gjerstad, Ole, ed. *Guinea-Bissau: Toward Final Victory: Selected Speeches and Documents from PAIGC.* Richmond, B.C., Canada: LSM Press, 1974.

Rudebeck, Lars. *Guinea-Bissau: A Study of Political Mobilization.* Uppsala, Sweden: The Scandinavian Institute of African Studies, 1974.

Venter, Al J. *Report on Portugal's War in Guinea-Bissau.* Pasadena: Munger Africana Library, 1973.

The 1971 - 1973 volumes of the English-language edition of PAIGC's bulletin, *PAIGC Actualites,* are available from LSM Information Center, P.O. Box 2077, Oakland, CA. 94604, USA.

WRITINGS AND SPEECHES BY AMILCAR CABRAL

Revolution in Guinea. London: Stage I, 1969 and New York: Monthly Review Press, 1973. (Edited by Richard Handyside.)

Our People Are Our Mountains. London: Committee for Freedom in Mozambique, Angola and Guine, n.d.

Return to the Source. New York: Africa Information Service, 1973.

Unite et lutte. Paris: Maspero, 1975. (two volumes.)

CURRENT INFORMATION

The journal *People's Power in Mozambique, Angola and Guinea-Bissau* is published bimonthly by the Mozambique, Angola and Guine

Information Center (MAGIC), 34 Percy Street, London WIP, 9FG, England. This center also publishes other current documentation from Guinea-Bissau and the other former Portuguese colonies.

General information can be obtained through the Guinea-Bissau Representative to the United Nations, 211 East 43rd Street, New York, N.Y. 10017, USA or directly from the Ministry of Information and Tourism, C.P. 191, Bissau, Republic of Guinea-Bissau.

Materials in Portuguese are available also from *Centro de Informacao e Documentacao Amilcar Cabral* (CIDAC); Rua Pinheiro Chagas, 77º-2 Esq.; Lisbon, Portugal.

More on Guinea-Bissau from LSM Press...

Guinea-Bissau: Toward Final Victory!

Selected Speeches and Documents from PAIGC

Here is the story behind the liberation struggle, incorporating writings and speeches by Amilcar Cabral and documents from PAIGC. Selections by Cabral include a class analysis of Guinean society, the role of culture in the revolution, and the changing role of women. Party documents and interviews cover other aspects of the liberation movement's history and political views. 1974. 98 pages, map, photos. $1.50

Write for a free catalog of our many publications on Africa and the Middle East.

Subscribe to LSM News

QUARTERLY JOURNAL OF LIBERATION SUPPORT MOVEMENT

Featuring reports and analysis on national liberation struggles and developments in the anti-imperialist movement.

standard subscription	$3
libraries and institutions	$6
first class postage	add $1
airmail postage (outside N. America)	add $5

LSM Information Center
P.O. Box 2077, Oakland, CA, 94604, USA